'A HEAD TA

Developing a Humanising Curriculum
Through Drama

Edited by

T. Grady
Hodge Hill School, Birmingham, UK

C. O'Sullivan
Newman College, UK

Technical Editor

T.M. Hayes
The University of Birmingham, UK

natd The National Association
for the Teaching of Drama

Invitations were based on presentations and workshops from the Conference entitled 'A Head Taller' - Developing a Humanising Curriculum through Drama, held at Newman College, Birmingham, 27 -29 June 1997.

British Cataloguing in Publication Data

A catalogue record for this book is available from the British Library

ISBN 0 946573 04 2

First Published in 1998 by The National Association for the Teaching of Drama, 69 Rookery Road, Selly Oak, Birmingham, B29 7DG, UK.

Designed and Typeset by Tom Hayes
Printed by The University of Birmingham, Edgbaston, Birmingham, B15 2TT, UK.

Gift 10

WITHDR

Contents

Foreword
Tony Grady and Carmel O'Sullivan   v

'Like Sisyphus We Keep Pushing at the Mountain'
Dorothy Heathcote   1

Mantle of the Expert
Iona Towler-Evans   14

Teacher in Role for Beginners
Kate Katiafiasz   22

Contexts Between Play, Drama, and Learning
Luke Abbott and Brian Edmiston   25

Story into Drama
Paul Kaiserman   35

Cross-Curricular Approaches to Drama in the Primary Classroom
Carmel O'Sullivan   42

Reaching Out: Ethical Spaces and Drama
Brian Edmiston   58

The *Full* Range of Culture?
Jonothan Neelands   70

Art as a Mode of Knowing
Louise Townend   78

Research and the Teaching of Drama
John Somers 87

Opening the Gap and Inserting the Contradiction
Bogusia Matusiak-Varley 96

Humanising GCSE
Guy Williams 109

The New Drama 'A' Level
Pauline Marson 115

The Meeting Point Between Drama and Text: Thoughts from a Workshop
Fiona Lesley 119

First Encounters with *Alchemy*, and Queer Goings-On in *The Cherry Orchard*
Brian Woolland 123

Grasping the Nettle Where it Stings Most
Geoff Gillham 133

Foreword

This collection of papers and articles is published following the 1997 Annual Conference of the National Association for the Teaching of Drama (United Kingdom). The conference set out to provide participants with the practical and theoretical understanding necessary to facilitate the development of a humanising, child-centred curriculum. Participants in the conference were invited to explore the tension between the current utilitarian demands of the British National Curriculum, and the commitment of many teachers to maintain and develop sound progressive educational theory and practice. The conference deliberately brought together differences, aiming to provide a productive context in which these differences could be better understood.

The material here represents a mixture of keynote addresses, notes on workshops, and more detailed analyses by workshop leaders of their practice and of the thinking behind that practice.

The collection begins with a piece by Dorothy Heathcote, where she asks readers to consider first the disarmingly simple questions, 'What's a good school?' and 'What's your ideal school?' Then, bringing us right up to date and pushing us to consider the actuality in which our children live: 'What does 'doing well' mean in the context of the realities of the cultural world children now are bringing into school with them?' She is keen to dispel the typical image of the teacher of drama as being 'highly suspect' in schools: "the barnacle attached to the ship of serious learning whose subject may lead children into slack ways of studying". She suggests ways of talking with colleagues in schools, drawing on 'hard theorists' to communicate the inconvertible argument that drama can educate for 'self-direction and self-realisation'.

The next five contributions focus clearly on classroom practice, some describing extensive practices with specific teaching and learning aims, others focusing on particular aspects of methodology.

These are followed by contributions from two of the conference's keynote speakers. In the first, Brian Edmiston makes a case for the centrality of ethics in classroom practice, especially in drama. He describes the potential power of drama to nurture our ethical selves and speaks about the importance of looking *beneath the facts* to discover questions which are worth pursuing. Jonothan Neelands distinguishes between natural and cultural in terms of understanding conceptions of living. He compares this differentiation with the literary and class-restricted cultural conception of the difference between theatre and drama. Neelands takes issue with the definition of culture given in the Association's policy document, arguing for the acceptance of a definition of cultures which emphasises the multiplicity of cultures, rather than a definition which encompasses a whole human culture. Louise Townend's article, reprinted from SCYPT Journal 32 (Summer, 1996), is the only piece in this publication not originating at the Conference. Townend provides an example of the theory underlying drama and theatre as ways of knowing the world. Through an analysis of the devising process for a Theatre in Education programme, she argues that the process of 'coming to know' can be sharpened through the practice of drama in education. In the following article, John Somers supports this approach of underpinning practice with sound theoretical perspectives, and he suggests possible ways to propagate a research culture amongst drama teachers which will serve to support, revitalise and develop the theory and practice of drama.

B. Varley, writing from the perspective of an experienced drama practitioner and an Ofsted Inspector, attempts to identify those aspects of good practice in drama in education which satisfy the demands placed on schools by the inspection system and suggests ways in which a Drama Department might approach the experience of inspection. She indicates that one of the criteria which Ofsted look for in an inspection is whether drama has an impact on standards in other subjects. Teachers encouraged by Somers in the previous article to undertake their own research, would be well equipped to support claims for their subject area in an inspection.

The next four articles return us to classroom practice, concentrating this time on practice with older students, particularly those taking examinations in drama. Some innovative approaches to the study of texts are suggested here and the writers build upon experiences that students might have had earlier in their experience of drama.

Finally, Geoff Gillham describes a 'practical keynote' in which conference participants began to question and reflect upon their experiences in schools *now*, thus enabling us to return to a consideration of the questions posed at the beginning by Dorothy Heathcote.

Taken together, the contributions offer a rich insight into drama in education as practised today by people working (for the most part) in the United Kingdom. They also represent the range of work being done, both in terms of the different age groups represented and the different geographical areas being worked in. More than that, though, they provide evidence of the integrity with which many teachers are still working: an integrity which shows in their concern to find ways of helping young people understand challenging subject matter.

It is important, too, that these contributions are seen in the context of recent changes to education in the United Kingdom, particularly in England and Wales. Since the passing of the 1988 Education Act, the concept of child-centred education has been under sustained attack. Successive governments have continued to undermine the teaching profession, and the results of these prolonged attacks are alarming.

In 1989, NATD published a booklet, *The Fight for Drama; the Fight for Education,* following a large conference which had debated the association's stance towards the then new Education Act. The association decided then to call for its repeal and this policy was re-affirmed after debate at the 1997 conference. It would have been hard to predict, in 1988, how far things would have gone in less than ten years.

Over this period, drama has been under fire in a number of different ways in the United Kingdom. The curriculum as a whole has shifted to a more utilitarian model and there has been consistent pressure from central government to replace any sort of exploratory, meaningful learning with regimented doctrines handed down to teachers. The intense focus on assessment, reporting and recording has taken teachers away from the business of *teaching* to 'compulsive' measuring of children's abilities in standardised testing. Because changes have occurred incrementally (but relentlessly), matters which might have once been hotly debated are now passively accepted. Teachers have gradually been dispossessed of the ability to think or speak about the fundamentals of education. In the case of younger teachers, their training was 'reformed' before they could ever consider such things.

Drama was excluded from the National Curriculum, then appeared as part of the English syllabus and occasionally, rather vaguely, as a cross-curricular tool serving the needs of other subjects. Theatre in Education, as a properly funded service to schools and local authorities has all but disappeared. Economic cutbacks and manufactured competition between schools through the use of crude league tables of examination results have led schools to concentrate on what are worryingly known as 'the basics' - literacy and numeracy (which, far from being 'basic' - in the sense of 'simple' - are actually among the most sophisticated tools developed by humanity). Drama's educational methodology, relying, as it does, on a <u>social</u> exploration of phenomena, does not fit with the individualised approach to learning now favoured in British schools. Its ability to investigate the whole of something, through working on a particular and moving to examine universal layers of meaning, is the opposite of what is encouraged in a fragmented and fragmentary curriculum. And this fragmented and fragmentary curriculum is causing our children to fail to learn. They are not encouraged to think or question but have become digesters of rigidly prescribed syllabi in what Paulo Freire (1972) calls 'the banking concept of education'. He points to narration as being the dominant emphasis in education, which leads to information becoming lifeless and static - mechanical memorisation. This method of education as an act of *depositing* rather than *communicating* instills passivity in students, denying them the possibility of developing a critical consciousness which would result from their intervention of the world as transformers of it. We need to fight against the current situation where students accept a fragmented view of reality that is *deposited* in them. This concept of education minimises creativity, which further enforces the disempowerment of our young people. Sartre (1947) has also written about this concept of depository knowledge which he calls the 'digestive' or 'nutritive' concept of education, in which knowledge is fed by the teacher to the students to 'fill them out'. Heathcote here cites James Moffett (1995) who insists on a shift of emphasis from memorisation to higher-order thinking, and active students making decisions and constructing their own meaning: "promoting drive rather than passivity, independence rather than dependence, originality rather than conformity".

Many of our teachers, whilst remaining committed to the young people they teach and whilst working harder than teachers have ever worked, have lost the ability to reflect upon and analyse what they are doing. The National

Curriculum treats them as 'deliverers' of bits of knowledge and that is what they have become. Institutions where new teachers are trained have become trainers of deliverymen and women, and are turning out committed new teachers who are often unable to think how schools could be different. This has been deliberately engineered - that is why teacher training, both initial and in-service, has been made into a largely 'practical' matter, why theory has been deliberately removed from courses.

The conference which generated these papers set out consciously to examine what we do when we are faced with working in this context. We would assert that in doing so, it was the most important educational conference to take place in the last twelve months, in that it reminded us that things do not have to be as they are. We are told that there has been much debate about education in recent years. Sadly, most of it has been debate based on the assumption that the present system needs to be made to work better. NATD would argue differently. The present system needs to be changed - radically. Freire (1972) sees education and critical pedagogy as a cultural praxis to lift the ideological veil in people's consciousness, which will reverse the current utilitarian ideology where "The educated [person] is the adapted [person] because s/he is better 'fit' for the world". Teachers need to dismiss this 'ready to wear approach' which obviates thinking and questioning. Freire (1972) warns that one of the gravest obstacles to the achievement of liberation [humanisation] "is that oppressive reality absorbs those within it and thereby acts to submerge [people's] consciousness. Functionally, oppression is domesticating". We would argue that drama in education allows the learner to emerge from such domesticity and turn upon it, which as Freire argues can "only be done by means of the praxis: reflection and action upon the world in order to transform it". He believes that it is only possible to understand the contradictions in society if the learner confronts reality critically, objectifying it and acting upon that reality.

Ironically, the number of secondary students opting to take the subject rises year by year. The ability that young people have to dramatise is probably their real 'basic skill', developing, as it does, from children's play. It is clear from the contributions printed here that it is a powerful method of learning in many curriculum areas. This book is, we believe, a testament to what can be achieved by teachers and students who can develop elements of play into elements of drama. That is one definition of a child-centred education - that we begin with the child and with what the child knows and can do. That we then work in a way which enables a group of children collectively to bring their 'old' knowledge to a new, human encounter in such a way that they will, individually and collectively, develop 'new' knowledge, thus leaving the encounter 'a head taller'. We do not know of any other association of teachers which is attempting this. That is why we are able to assert that the conference which generated these papers was the most important educational conference to take place in Britain in the last twelve months.

Tony Grady and Carmel O'Sullivan
viii

References

Freire, P. (1972). *Pedagogy of the Oppressed.* Translated by Myra Bergman Ramos. London: Sheed and Ward.

McLaren, P. and Leonard, P. (eds.) (1993). Paulo Freire. A Critical Encounter. London: Routledge.

Sartre, J. P. (1947). 'Une idée fundamentale de la phénomenologie de Husserl: L'intentionalité', *Situations 1* , Paris.

Notes

We have endeavoured to intervene as little as possible with individual authors' styles in an effort to maintain the original voice and emphasis in a spirit of respect for and acknowledgment of difference, which was one of the important goals of the conference.

'Like Sisyphus We Keep Pushing at the Mountain'

Dorothy Heathcote

Dorothy Heathcote is the President of NATD.

I feel I have a bit of a cheek in pontificating having been out of the mainstream of schools and schooling for some years now. Not that one stops thinking and wishing one could change the world. Ever since I began thinking about schools and drama and teaching, I've been pondering on just what the blockage is which makes the mainstream school system have to struggle to get children interested in whatever subject areas are currently in fashion. They never seem to look seriously at <u>motivation</u>. Common sense and your own experience tells you that short exposure to a variety of academic subjects is a poor recipe for committed involvement!

Most days even now I wonder why such an outmoded system is so hung on to. Schools are like no other places on the planet. A place set aside, supposedly to make it special for the young and easier to concentrate on the menu presented, seems self defeating, when the system, talk and demeanour is antiseptic. Teacher talk in the main can seem less than inspiring if the content no sooner gets going than it all changes to another subject. Sometimes I think I have a kind of answer regarding why we hang on to this paradigm of children as vessels to be filled up as well as possible and then be asked to take it out again and sort it into the sort of knowledge which is supposed to empower them for life as mature, productive, authentic members of our culture. You may find my answer a bit simplistic. I think we're afraid of the classes getting out of hand. Children in groups can be fearsome. Yet when you follow children through the various stages of their schooling it's plain to see a teacher-dependent system is bound to run into problems.

It must dawn on all children at some stage that what happens outside school is not relevant, or seems not to be, to what happens inside classrooms and vice versa. People like I was, loved school, and the reasons were many and various. First, being poor (and I really mean that), to me the teachers seemed like beings from another planet. They wore silk blouses, had beads and nice handbags. The men teachers wore shoes not boots and three piece suits and ties. They (the women anyway) seemed genteel and didn't speak in dialect. It was nice to be in school in their company, for in the main they dealt kindly towards us.

Then there was the work. Lots of different things to learn about, and if like me, you had a good memory; it was pretty comfortable. And the books, oh the books: occasional coloured pictures, maps, and black and white photographs of places like Niagara Falls. Even seeing the real thing later wasn't so awe inspiring as when I realised there was a tiny little boat right in the bottom of the picture amidst the mists. And the library box - 'The Mystery of the Swaying Curtains'

1

still curdles my blood!

And the bulbs growing in glass jars; beans and cress and peas in blotting paper and old strips of flannel. It didn't need to be like our lives outside school and it didn't seem antiseptic, for we knew that our teachers knew more, knew it better and knew what was good for us. Harriet Findlay Johnson's school in Little Sompting differed little from my schooling even though she was teaching over thirty years earlier. No wonder I took to her when I found her book.

You only had to be told that the policeman or the school attendance man or a teacher was 'looking out for you' for a sort of fainting fear to come over you. So in the main you were good. Looking back it seems a splendid mystery turned me on to school, and when I meet my old classmates (we're getting thinner on the ground!), we still seem to share the same feelings about our school days-daze?

All this preamble is leading me to a simple thought but one which I believe to be accurate. Whenever I'm due to teach a class I bring it to the forefront of my mind. I find it easy to subdue my own immediate interests and go with the teacher's current concerns. It doesn't seem a sacrifice. Some children still seem willing and able to do that, but our contemporary children come into school bursting with a range of stimulating, somehow urgent and nervy experiences, and see no reason why their concerns should be less important than those of teachers and schools. They know teachers are not Gods though they may be aliens! Beads and handbags don't fill them with awe. They know what teachers earn and the sort of homes they live in. There's rightly, less awe about.

Our outside school experiences were equally vivid to us as those of today's children. We were able to spend much time in the streets, in the fields (hay time and great horses) making dens, cricket in the alleyways, gathering flowers and berries in season, Sunday school, church choir, girl guides and bilberrying. And the older generations were all intermingled, sitting around the lanes and talking in yards. You may think I lived a childhood like Tess of the D'urbervilles, but safer! I need to constantly revisit these memories when I meet the current school population. In their 'country' I am as the blind. I cannot, try as I may, know the territory and pace of their interior and out of school experiences. I need to pay very close attention to their behaviour, eye contact with myself, treatment of things and each other. These are the only clues I have about motivating their interest.

Between my childhood and taking up my work in the university at twenty four there was a war: images on film changed and the world of children was already to me less sharply understood. Since that time there has been a succession of radical changes all adding to the confusion of the adult about how children see and perceive their world. There have been a variety of theories about how children learn, shifts in curriculum priorities, and discourse about teaching styles. This dream of returning to an earlier time of school discipline, children's willingness to submit to tidy classroom behaviours is a myth. Yet teachers are being bombarded with usually useless and insensitive help. Deep in our hearts we know we've lost the battle of telling our information to children, and

2

criminally (in my view) we prepare new (and brave) teachers to work in increasingly unhelpful circumstances. You don't need me to list these.

We thought we were enfranchising children and we still think so. But we haven't. We've done what all people in establishments do, we change the rules but the old laws still operate. Our children know the rules - (you can't lay a finger on me; I know my rights; you're only a teacher). The laws however, still operate which prevent school being a really maturing experience. We don't trust ourselves and our pupils to develop working relationships whereby students can assume real responsibility within the system. Teacher dependence, if not necessarily overt, is still a covert factor. I would hope that no teacher would deliberately set out to keep their charges in thrall to them. The problem lies with the trailing encumbrances attached to the role of student when linked with the word teacher. Through the ages since formal schooling started, when the curriculum began to be taught detached from the practical working life, this has remained a problem in the development of student responsibility for outcomes. It establishes a mind set. Further there is a certain lack of trust in the capacity of children to behave decently in crowds. A small classroom and a collection of large (and sometimes smallish!) people can feel like a crowd when there is mischief afoot. The terms teacher and pupil can militate against the capacity to be self-motivating in school as they often prove they can be when they leave the school gates each day.

One of the problems lies in the way learning situations split the day. When I taught in university I was constantly amazed at the way the timetable was arranged for those aspiring to be teachers. The day being divided into short sessions seemed contrary to the message being covertly implied - that integrated days seemed more conducive to learning. The day divided into subjects isn't really about learning or the curriculum. In secondary schools, it's about making certain the teaching load is fairly divided and all subject teachers get a fair chance to impart their subject. Short periods save teachers from dealing with difficult-to-motivate classes who may get out of hand, even though most children still accommodate to it. It's the one or two in any artificially composed group who will not set aside their interests and needs at the behest of the teacher. They're the ones who are not afraid to declare their interests, stage of maturity and personalities. The conformers have these but are prepared to veil them temporarily, try to use school time productively and wait for their real lives to take over at breaktimes. If you think this is nonsense look at the curve of interest as it rises and falls at different stages throughout the schooling years. In school the little ones exchange their out of school family parent for the teacher mother/father. Teachers of young juniors are revered for a while as they organise the variety of experiences of the school day, and fairly distribute the classroom resources and their own selves in the interests of the individual children. Most teachers of young junior children appear to parents as they listen to their off spring, to be paragons of virtue compared with themselves!

But then the day becomes not only divided into sections of time, but different teachers each with individual styles as they approach their subject, have to be accommodated to. This is a problem for staff and pupils. The one has to overcome group inertia as children switch focus, and the other has to accommodate to information, teacher personality and kind of attention and brain function required. This happens co-incidentally with the period when students are beginning to be critical observers of adults, and that can blind students to the realisation that most teachers would love to share their knowledge and pleasure in their subject with their pupils.

When the number of subjects narrows there is often a change in the relationship. With more time to be spent, in smaller groups displaying more social health, teacher and students can achieve a more authentic relationship with (hopefully) more mutual respect and responsibility. This is the time when the lucky ones can develop productive obsession from a variety of motives. Genuine interest in the subject, maybe realising the teacher is interested (and interesting), wanting to 'do well', to please others, sensing freedoms to come; all may be aspects which influence a responsible attitude coming into school along with the school books. Pupils of all these ages and stages pass my gate morning and afternoon and these shifts of attitude are easily recognised.

I haven't written a single word you don't already know before. I seem to have been knocking on the door of motivating students to enjoy responsibility for years and years. The establishment seems not to have faced this problem one iota differently since I was a child. But children are changed utterly since then, in what experiences they carry into school from a society and culture which <u>has</u> changed. A small example which happened today in the Metro on the way to Newcastle. Two sixteen year old girls on the last day of this school year. One strips a plastic wrapper off a gooey stick of something edible, licks it to get the last dregs of flavour, and defying me with a long hard stare tucks it into the seat to soil someone else's clothes when they sit down. That sounds like a carping grumble but it's the hard stare from the two girls who looked interesting, pretty and charming, till the values of two generations are activated which makes one want to bridge that gap, at least in the hours of school. I know that miracles of class interest, responsibility and decent mutual respect must happen each day in a variety of school locations, but frequently the establishment (if it notices) puts it down to individual talent in teachers or the special nature of the subject. And that way they don't have to change the old order.

The new government is still upholding it also. In the past six weeks, when yet more changes are urged upon teachers, never once have I heard the words 'motivate students' spoken. And that applies to the teachers' union leaders as well as the minister and his minions. It's time people like members of NATD and such organisations begin to show that their subject area deals with motivating people <u>as they are</u> in school; that it invites participation which does not subdue the real social and intellectual readiness of students. That it contains the possibility of reflection about cultural dimensions during active participation. But above all it can by its nature, shift the frame of reference and point of view by which students enter the classroom work. Put bluntly, role shifts and behaviours can be tried out and tested by making contracts, so that all participants, including the class leader, agree that it's a pretence for now but is truthful to the

4

circumstances deliberately set up for enquiry, whether it be academic or cultural.

To do the above demands that class leaders develop many strategies for interesting and motivating students to invest themselves in the matter in hand intellectually. The secret of motivating thus lies in the spiritual element which has to be activated when people identify themselves from within an event. Spirituality is not religion. It is the vital invisible spark without material substance which begins to have sacred significance. Whenever we meet purposeful enthusiasm, 'stickability', drive for engagement with tasks and interest in information, we know we have motivated students. To do this demands many techniques. When children are small, their social skills are tenuous so strategies which help them to succeed in spite of this are necessary. A language of reflections in action has to be won, so further and different teaching skills are necessary. Later, overcoming of embarrassment among peers becomes essential as also protection from feeling stared at has to engage the teacher/leader's negotiating skills. In how many classrooms do you find these highly detailed strategies at work? And how often are they seriously discussed at staff meetings? I mean in fine detail. The use of voice, vocabulary, tone, style; the way material is prepared for 'engagement' and lure of student interest; and the environment deliberately and subtly changed for different kinds of engagement. (I'm not discussing decorations or new furniture either!) You who work in drama approaches for learning know you have to be flexible and skilled in all these, even if you're not entirely satisfied with your own use of them. Because you know that shifting students from "let's learn about this subject" to "let's participate in *now* involving all of our experience in meeting and identifying with people who have need of knowledge of this 'subject' " is not merely a matter of opening books, or looking at a picture or listening to a teacher transmitting information, though all these examples will be used when appropriate. To engage participation from within, a different responsibility, a changed mind set, a challenge to resolution, requires that a teacher/leader becomes an inventor of strategies relevant to the students' willingness, resistance, social health, rivalry of peers and state of mind regarding their last lesson and cultural attitudes. Such creative teachers constantly re-invent themselves. And they need not be teachers of drama. But in our culture it is often those working in drama who have passed a rubicon, a cultural block involving expressive behaviour which goes beyond the 'normal' expected of teachers in classrooms where talk is the main medium of communication. The teacher of drama is seen often as shape-shifter and thus highly suspect or specially gifted. The trouble is that it permits us to be sidelined.

We are seen as the playmakers, the deliberate hobbyists, the barnacle attached to the ship of serious learning whose subject may lead children into slack ways of studying. Sports teachers, musicians, art teachers, the erstwhile versions of wood and metal work teachers and those in domestic science can be seen to be more serious, more earth bound, more useful because they all use specialised and sometimes dangerous equipment. But your drama teacher who may be using equally risky stuff (electricity!) is still making illusion. And people don't die if there's no continued make believe - OR DO THEY? The old arguments haven't convinced many of our colleagues, though I occasionally hear that 'so and so seems to be behaving a bit differently in class' after some drama event. There'll have to be another line of persuasion found, and it seems to me to lie in this area of capacity to motivate people to study, which dramatic approaches can offer. But you can't sell it if your skills are not honed and your interests must be seen to lie in intellectual development based in spirituality. We need a better word for our materialistic age. 'Feeling' frightens the horses and hasn't convinced the establishment as being useful and essential to academic development. 'Creative learning' sounds airy fairy. So I'm going to suggest another way of talking with colleagues.

Forgive this short apparent deviation. When I was wondering what NATD committee had in mind when they asked me to 'say a few words' - as if that were possible for such as I - a few things happened which together brought about a serendipity of focus.

Ted Wragg (1997) had suggested a possible curriculum development in the form of a cube diagram. Gavin [Bolton] spotted that there was no reference to learning in context other than the usual "we're in school to learn". He too had written to the Professor [Wragg] intimating that the approach to context can be achieved using a Mantle of the Expert approach. The reply he received was courteous and somewhat dismissive even though Gavin had showed how such a contextual approach can shift the frame or point of view by which students enter the area of study and thus be empowered and motivated towards the curriculum.

Then I heard two Tyneside ladies in the metro train discussing how one of their relatives had got one of their children into 'a good school'. So what's a good school seemed appropriate for NATD members to contemplate.

Later a visitor from Canada closing an interview with me asked about "the constituents of your ideal school". So what's an ideal school?

Then Raymond Williams on Radio 4 was discussing Hardy's *Return of the Native* and quoted from it: "Mother, what does 'doing well' mean?" These three very basic and simple (seeming) statements seem to me to be matters of great urgency to be discussed in relation to our current culture and human world problems. How may considering these give teachers who use drama different arguments, though still based in their belief in their field and without compromising that knowledge.

Then, through further serendipity I came across James Moffett's (1994) *The Universal School House. Spiritual Awakening Through Education.* His book seems to present you with respectable, well established arguments related with motivation and drama strategies. So I shall quote from this book from now on, hoping it may arm you with an 'establishment' vocabulary backed by the most respected writers on education and schooling. Moffett (1994) himself being a highly respected scholar and classroom practitioner champions the kind of work you do (if you do it well of course!) in invoking a spiritual and user-friendly basis for the school work anticipated in current curriculum design. He shows by example, backed by quotations and references to many academic theorists and thinkers in the field of formal schooling, how such working practice forms a central engine to academic study. His cogent argument stresses rigour, a variety of skills, and forms of approach which he names. Moffett (1994) doesn't plead for the arts as a basis for motivated study. He advances an inconvertible argument that committed learning depends on the thinking brain where proof, evidence and detailed exploration of factual material requires to be generated on a background of feeling and being locked into previous experience of students. To sustain his arguments he uses Bruner, Wordsworth (giving a superb analysis of 'The Intimations of Immortality from Recollections of Early Childhood'), Montessori, Dewey, Whitehead, Read, Chomsky, Skinner, Steiner, the Resinks, Frank Smith, Howard Gardner - the persuasive 'frame' man, Suzanne Langer, Fromm, Erikson, Campbell, Mercia Iliade, Levi Strauss and more. Now these are 'hard' theorists, names your colleagues will have been brought up on during their teacher preparation. There aren't any references to the equally 'hard' thinkers from the current arts world to frighten the horses and put you back among the cranks! I'm suggesting that you discuss your contribution to the life of your school, whatever the age of the children attending it from the point of view of methods and ways of teaching, not the subject itself. And please don't bring up the hoary pleading for including theatre studies. They are included and the laws of that art form are integral to all interactions involving change of frame as an aid to motivating students to study. Cauldwell Cook taught Shakespeare's plays through such a shift: by all agreeing that they were actors in a company of the period of The Globe and The Swan. And that's years ago, so change of frame as an aid to study is well established.

Now you must harness your thoughts around my three questions: What's a good school? What's your ideal school? and What does 'doing well' mean in the context of the realities of the cultural world children now are bringing into school with them? This is the basic foundation of school staffrooms - well, let's hope it is. The ladies in the metro gave homely child-centred answers, though it doesn't follow that they applied them in their dealings with children. 'They come home happy. They talk about school. They seem to thrive on what they've been doing in school. They bring things home. They take things in. They settle to and take care over their homework. They say when they're worried.' Oh, and they liked the idea of uniforms as levellers regarding income, not status of the school. Their statements seem to have a basis in Moffett's spirituality, the vital numinous spark. But in staffrooms among your professional colleagues you have to unpick the portmanteau words such as happy, talk about, thrive, bring home, take out, settle to, take care, worried. Getting the implications of 'happy' into a careful breakdown of classroom practices is a labour of Hercules. It involves not only a precise agreed 'hard' definition but analysis of what kinds of experiences incubate it and then each colleague has to agree to keep such experiences active, each in their own way, every minute, hour and day they are in child contact, plus minute monitoring of children's behaviour in response. And 'happy' is only one of the words. What about *stretching* children, challenging, supporting, sharing responsibility? Sisyphus and his rock rolling is simpler to achieve.

Our ladies in the metro gave child centred examples of a good school.

7

My colleagues at the university listed standards related with the work done in school. Quite understandable because most parents can't imagine in detail how teaching takes place. Their clearest images relate to when they were pupils attending school. But colleagues get into classrooms, so they list 'full-potential, stretched, progression, set homework, school organisation, discipline, learning how to study and application'. I can't argue with any of these. But what is progress? How do you define it in your work? How do you recognise it? How can you test for it?

Ted Wragg's cube sketch in The Guardian (1997) posited the kinds of learning outcomes based in the experience gained in classroom learning encounters. What are some possible encounters which arise from working through a drama component? We say *social* encounters - what do we really mean and how do we explain in hard detail what we mean? We say it demands collaboration, exploring culture - its history and evolving future, empathy, the behaviour of people and the way they are behaving in social circumstances styled by fictional pressure and the variety of theatre forms available to us in the classrooms. Our work involves an adult's experience, information and knowledge meeting the experience and behaviour of younger people in deliberately contrived events, tightly woven to enable productive tension and resolution (for the time) during immediate praxis-reflection in action. This demands a wide range of kinds of encounters not just amongst the participants, but with books and information, works of art involving a wide variety of materials, reading and writing in many styles. Your average school classroom involves a few tasks as the basis of most learning encounters. Listening, looking, reading, writing, discussing, observing, being observed. These form the action of most classrooms and they continue through many years. I do not denigrate them, they're useful ways to get to know things but how are they used if 'knowing and realising what you know' are intended? Each one requires a different organisation of tasks for that. So today's teachers involved in the current curriculum are faced with designing tasks which recognise the cultural experiences of today's youth. Not the time of my youth, nor even the time of your youth, but this day's immediate, vibrant, nervy, secretive (we've built a youth culture remember!) lot. They are just as capable of respect, dreaming, aspirations, compassionate behaviour as we think we were but it has to be released to inform all the other attitudes.

Moffett (1995, 105) reminds us what was suggested at the famous Dartmouth seminar in the early seventies - "The conference proposed:
- Accommodation of individual differences in background and learning modality
- Active students making decisions and constructing their own meaning
- Considerable interaction among students
- Heterogeneous classes
- Integration of all the language arts
- Looser boundaries between ages and between subjects
- Shift of emphasis from memorization to higher-order thinking

- Assessment in full accord with the highest goals
- Learning of language particles via whole texts and speech acts
- Greater development of oral language, as in dramatic work.

Most schools are still very far from actually implementing this excellent programme, which was delayed twenty years because the Dartmouth recommendations were stymied by governmental determination to impose behaviorally objectified evaluation and accountability."

Do you see much of this happening? Do you in your drama work engage it? Because if you do then this is how you need to talk about it with colleagues: "researchers list over a dozen ways in which schooling could foster self-education. It would, for example, help students to:

- 'Internalise control over their own learning'
- 'Identify and become expert at the activity or activities that may become central in their lives'
- Integrate 'theoretical studies with technical training and practical application ... for specific use now rather than learning for possible use years later'
- 'Generate their own goals rather than ... pursue goals set for them by others'
- 'See themselves successfully experiencing very desirable attainments ... and plan an effective way of making that vision a reality'
- Engage in 'patterns of exploration' and 'try out a wide range of fields of activities'
- 'Develop a personal learning style'
- 'Identify themes emerging in their lives, to build on those they choose, and to create new themes they desire'
- 'Not only master some knowledge or skill, but also .... develop a healthy attitude toward themselves, others, the world, and their activities'.

Teaching for self-education involves:
- 'Promoting drive rather than passivity, independence rather than dependence, originality rather than conformity'
- 'Training in the process skills, such as reading and remembering, especially at the moment students urgently need to gain access to information'
- 'Creating an active environment in which a student's self-directed activities are warmly supported and there are many opportunities to form close working relationships'.

The double emphasis on self-direction and social grounding accords well with my own recommendations. Indeed, all of these conditions for self-teaching would naturally be a part of the communal learning network, since they feature individual opportunities to find and develop oneself and to gain timely access to all available human and material resources. 'Learning how to learn' often appears among the lofty goal statements of school districts, but setting the conditions for real self-teaching means transforming public education", (Moffett, 1994, 197-8).

Now look at Moffett's (1994) list of classroom interactions and forms of encountering learning. As you examine each one, consider when and if you use it, and how and why.

Witnessing (not just staring, but the Biblical 'I bear witness')

Self teaching	Transmitting	Mentoring*
Imitating	Apprenticing	Taking stock
Helping	Interning	Rippling*
Collaborating	Coaching	Interacting
Visiting	Experimenting	Gaming

* see Moffett (1994)

These forms of learning are not the only ones available I realise, but they involve the whole person amongst their peers, that's why they are useful to you in giving examples to colleagues to explain how your work is closely related to theirs. Look at collaborating related with coaching; look at apprenticing and interacting. How many precise examples have you set up this past week? What context, what content, and to what ends? What is role work if it doesn't involve visiting and encountering? The problem of the list for your colleagues is these words don't seem to have anything to do with the earlier and shorter list where academic products and processes are plain to see. Do your classes write as a natural part of the work? Do they read, if so what, how much and why? The trouble is that when colleagues pass your classes they often don't see overt academic practices where precise recording, calculating, working with text (other than play texts) can be seen as natural to your kind of work.

Moffett (1994, 167-9) has this to say about rippling and mentoring, and it seems very relevant to me related with drama strategies.

"Rippling - Constrained as they have been, however, schools have not availed themselves of what may well be the most powerful learning method of all, because age grouping works against it, and because the managerial systems built into curriculum packages would eliminate themselves were they to accommodate it. I will call this method *rippling*. Basically, it's an informal, continuous tutorial of some knowledge or skill that everybody is at once receiving from the more experienced and transmitting in turn to the less experienced. ... This way of learning works consistently well across a variety of learners and subjects. Literacy could be entirely passed on in this folk fashion from those who read and write to those who don't. It's the main way many people have learned outside of school to do all sorts of arts, crafts, or sports or to operate everything from machines to offices and whole complicated businesses or other enterprises. Most adults learned how to do their jobs this way. It's the ripple effect.

Working with people who know more than you do and with those who know less can hardly be surpassed as a way to learn. Everybody benefits from and contributes to collective knowledge. Rippling is by nature individualized and interactive. It fits the learner and stays spontaneous, alive. It spiritualizes learning because everybody is giving to everybody else and helping each other realize themselves."

You are engaging classes in rippling when you bring in other age groups to learn by working alongside each other. If ever whole schools value rippling the whole structure of the timetable and enfranchisement of children will shift. I've seen eleven year old children showing GCSE students "who else might be around, and what might they be doing" when Polonius is bidding farewell to Horatio. The young ones working from studying paintings of docks of different periods and in different parts of the world, and the older using their understanding of the bonding between Horatio and his father to fit in and around all the 'stuff of action' brought by the younger ones learning to penetrate paintings. It all ripples backwards and forwards as they mentor each other. Moffett (1994, 190) states:

"Finding and working with mentors should indeed figure prominently in a communal learning network, but let's note that although the process may function at many levels of knowledge and intensity, the ratio between risk and gain remains. *From a mentor you learn by presence, both theirs and yours*; [my emphasis] otherwise get your expertise from a tutor, computer, book, lecture, or demonstration."

But what do all the participants then do in order to realise their new understanding? Aye, there's the rub. There is such a variety of curriculum work available because of the praxis, but do drama teachers take it to the next step? Do you?

What if each younger child works with an older child to produce (in writing/sketching/recording whatever is available) the internal text which the Shakespearean script must carry. Is this apprenticing? Is it visiting? Is it taking stock? And how may it be assessed? And how shall it be presented for examination by others? 'A written subtext with notes on the relationship between Horatio and his father Polonius' or 'The hazards of sea journeys in the Middle Ages, using evidence from art and Shakespeare's text of Hamlet' or 'Psychological undercurrents in Shakespeare's Hamlet with special reference to Polonius' advice to Horatio his son'. If you think it's far fetched I shouldn't bother reading more of this.

"If it seems extravagant to recommend that children be totally immersed in the arts as a first priority, consider the fundamental role the arts play in making things, whether objects or knowledge. Writing is making texts. As Frank Smith has documented and eloquently argued, literacy emerges from such personal construction. Creativity is not a sentimental or romantic concept; it is the most practical fact of human learning. Until we honor it, we will never make reading and writing a way of life so natural that education can assume literacy and go on to other things. The spiritual way is the practical way as much in learning to read and write as elsewhere. The language arts and the other arts engage the inner life with the physical

11

and social worlds. They partake of both mind and matter. In this sense, as incarnation, they are all soulful and best learned soulfully." (Moffett, 1994, 243)

You have a distinct advantage over your colleagues. You have probably been manufacturing your own teaching aids for years. You may use visiting roles, pictures, draped fabrics, the black board to sign and crystallise a space (for example, turning it into a pub sign, a notice of hanging, a declaration, a shop window, chemists' shelves, or a plan for a machine), home made name tags, cards for instructions, cards carrying photographs, cards with fragments of text, a card dictionary introducing the spelling of newly used vocabulary, to name just a few. You've probably, but it won't be seen as a virtue by traditional colleagues, broken your enslavement to THE TEXTBOOK, and so escaped what Moffett calls "the tyranny of dependence on publishers" (Moffett, 1994, 220).

Also you may not blanch so easily when asked to contemplate a long detailed project. Your constant re-framing of students as they enter a work session, working episodically, coming at curriculum from different aspects, viewpoints and modes of working. You may find it easier to ask the help of other teachers so that children can be better informed about a chosen area. When I was working with year ten in a project with Claire Armstrong-Mills at Primrose Hill School in Birmingham, we needed a straight academic lecture (but wearing his formal academic gown) from the Head of History to explain to the young doctors at Surgeon's Hall in the days of Dr Knox, why so many homeless vagrants were wandering Edinburgh and thus falling easy prey to the Infamous Burke and Hare. With the best will in the world, neither Claire nor I could provide the complexity of a historian's composite understanding. What we provided was a class of year tens who were working 'as if ' they were students of Dr Knox, short of corpses since the ending of the Napoleonic wars!

"Contrast the self-contained, prescheduled course given as a class with the story James Watkins tells in *The Double Helix* of how, in pressing forward to discover the DNA molecule, he turned aside temporarily to get tutored by a colleague in some math he had never had but required for the next stage of his problem solving, to which he returned provided with just what he needed when he needed it. *That's* how it has to happen - as part of a project, the natural unit for individualized, interactive, interdisciplinary learning.

Watson's framework was a project. Organizing around projects rather than around subjects will better teach the subjects, which need each other and a purposeful framework to realize themselves. This way of organizing education, furthermore, accommodates student-centred learning, because students conceive their own projects for some real-life purpose - to make something, investigate something, or improve something. As distinguished from a drill or exercise, which is done only in school, a project is an authentic act or series of acts complete for the purpose of the participants." (Moffett, 1994, 227).

So we're all in good company when we share teaching. James Watkins was already motivated to 'get some additional maths'. Our young doctors *became* motivated to listen to the history lecture as they needed to realise that doctors at that time required the dead in order to understand the human body in all its complexity of form and function. Moffett (1994, 240) refers to "the best learning takes place in a virtual trance", and goes on to say that "the primal function of participating in dance, music, drama, literature and visual arts I believe is trance induction. For the real learning that takes [place] and counts, one must *undergo* something in order to understand it. The arts are not mere things to learn but ways to learn" [my emphasis]. This is what we've known for years - that when you work in drama you're off guard, in a no-penalty zone.

The current tragedy for this generation when the whole of humanity is crying out for a new paradigm for schooling systems, is that even if we manage to prepare a new generation of teachers to break the mould, they have to work in schools which less and less function through a spiritual component to knowledge. Let Moffett (1994, 342) have the last words.

"Like a clutching parent who fears self-elimination if truly successful in bringing children to maturity, the culture does not really want its members to grow up, although it exists to benefit them. So the culture and individuals have to co-evolve. The reason that history shows a pattern of consciousness evolving from collective to individual may be that this direction does indeed fulfill a cosmic purpose. In any case it seems sensible for a culture to undertake today to wean individuals from itself if only to halt the slaughter and strife. This means deliberately educating for self-direction and self-realization. A new cosmopolitan kind of citizen will result who feels psychologically and spiritually self-sufficient enough to transcend ethnic and religious boundaries and put union over difference, cosmos over country or culture. Only then will the wars end."

References

Moffett, J. (1994). *The Universal School House. Spiritual Awakening Through Education.* Josey Bass Education Series: San Francisco, California.
Wragg, T. (1997). 'Countdown to the New Millennium.' *Guardian Education,* Tuesday April 8.

Mantle of the Expert

Iona Towler-Evans

Iona Towler-Evans is a curriculum advisor for Drama in Education in Dudley, the West Midlands.

"To most truly teach, one must converse; to truly converse is to teach."
(Thorp and Gallimore, 1988)

Of the many ingredients that make up the Mantle of the Expert system, the shift in teacher language and communication, for me, is one of the most essential and one of the most challenging.

Mantle of the Expert will demand that teachers and children 'truly converse', that their conversations are a genuine exchange of ideas where children grow to take responsibility for the work and learn to teach each other. Through these conversations, which may seem casual, the teacher will have carefully fed in useful information but without 'teacher telling'.

The spreading of responsibility is an important feature of Mantle of the Expert, where the teacher is always planning ways of discouraging teacher dependency but encouraging an investment from the children in what seems like real work carrying a real responsibility and commitment.

The children enter the functional roles of people who run an enterprise and through a series of incremental tasks learn the skills and understanding which build their expertise. The Mantle of the Expert is a way of teaching the curriculum but the skills and understanding developed and the knowledge encountered always arise from the context.

The authority which drives them is not the teacher, but the Enterprise and the client and the problems that need to be dealt with. If children are to function as Experts, then they must be treated as such but they also need the support from the structure which builds on their growing expertise. Sources of information have to be built into the structure so that the children interrogate these sources when they are needed. The teacher is not the only source of information and s/he has to select when to give information and how this information is received within an authèntic context. For example, in the enterprise about running a stable (which I introduced at the conference), if the teacher wants to alert the children to the dangers of too much Spring grass, s/he might introduce them to a task of checking charts detailing times/months/ stabling of horses or organising rotas for putting them in the starvation pen. The children will build their expertise through action, beginning with manageable tasks which do not expose their inexpertise but which allow them to operate as experts. Gradually, their tasks will become more complex.

Within this context the teacher will also adopt a functional role but will always adopt a collegiate relationship with the children, so instead of saying something like this,

"You see, when horses have too much Spring grass they could get colic, so we'll have to make sure we keep them off the grass"

s/he may say something like:

"Has anyone seen the vet's report on Molly? Was it colic? I know she'd been on that Spring grass a good while. What did the vet say when she came?"

The teacher in us will want them to understand the first explanation so we will tend to tell it like a teacher. The second example demonstrates a way of talking which gives the same information but allows the children to make the connections. It also allows the children to respond in an interactive way and perhaps, most importantly, it personalises knowledge.

The whole point is, that the children will gather understanding in context and will discover more as each episode develops. This will also move into action. Molly can be difficult to 'catch' (note the use of authentic language), and through the drama the group may collectively make attempts at attracting her to the stable. If you want the children to begin to work together the 'moving of Molly' will engage them in a collective problem. If you want the children to look at the implications of their responsibility they may need to explain to a horse owner the details of their horse's ailment and the procedures that have been taken. Running a stables can take you into several curriculum areas but in Mantle of the Expert it is the 'point of view' frame which colours how children learn and motivates them to discover new things. Knowledge is to be operated on by the children, not merely received. At the 'Interactive Drama Conference' held last year at UCE in Birmingham, Gavin Bolton remarked that "tying a knot as a boy scout is rather different from just tying a knot". In the same way, checking accident reports as a person running a stables who needs to be accountable for those accidents, is rather different from just checking accident reports.

In the workshop at the conference I introduced a way into the 'Running the Stables Enterprise', and together with the participants, reflected on the possibilities and implications of this way of working. The resources I prepared to support the structure included a pictorial map which I named 'The Old Well House Stables' (see Appendix I) and a letter regarding lottery funding in order that we could move to new and expanded premises. I thought it was important to establish our stables as ones which gave access to all kinds of people in the community and which had created 'horse-share' opportunities and so on, so that from the outset the main thrust of the stables was seen as working for the community, not for profit. These stables needed to have a special dimension. I introduced the Enterprise through a combination of teacher talk and visual resource (pictorial map). My aim was to demonstrate the shift in teacher language within Mantle of the Expert which eased the group into entering the fiction. For example,

"Often, they think people like you can't run big jobs [suggestion of a

challenge here] *but would you agree with me that if you were pushed we could run a market stall, buying, pricing, ...* [a hint of 'let's show them what we can do'] *Would you have a go with me at running a big enterprise? ...* [the teacher here is modelling courtesy - they are being asked] *I wonder whether you'd help me run a big stables ... we could give it a go if they trust us* [they will be accountable].

Of course, I'm just inventing this stable, wouldn't it be interesting if we did ... " [reminding them it's a fiction, but it will be a very truthful context].

I continued, during my talk to fill in the context but also to shift to a greater use of 'we' and 'us'.

"You see, we will be moving to a new stables eventually and we'd need to look at some possible sites but I was so pleased that they gave us the grant. They were very impressed with our links with the community, the way we involved the youngsters from the school and the Riding for the Disabled Scheme. [Possibilities here for written instructions for mounting the horse for young disabled riders who want to do so independently, as well as possibilities for designing a mounting block for a person who's lost the use of one leg.]

Last night, I started thinking back to the time when we first came to these stables. You remember all the problems we had, that well was a problem. Rocky always caught his head collar on it. Anyway, I drew this plan as well as I could, the way I remembered this place ... [this plan is described as one I drew. I couldn't pretend it was an architect's plan as this would lose the authenticity]. *Of course it's changed a bit since then. Now, we'll be starting all over again at the new place; I thought it might be helpful to remind ourselves of these things. I've also got the accident reports (see Appendix II), perhaps we could go through them and make a note of anything useful we need to think about when we move."*

Now, I've given them resources to look at so they don't feel stared at and they are learning through tasks that will begin to build their expertise but which will also support them. These resources are the non-negotiable elements in the drama which serve to support the teacher as well as the children. They help to establish agreements, they become the authority instead of the teacher, and they breed curriculum work and so help you teach it.

In this particular structure the following details were built in so most curriculum areas could be addressed. The pictorial map of the stables provided a good opportunity for including the details given in Table 1 (see overleaf) which would address the curriculum.

The accident reports detailed incidents which were partly due to the 'givens' on the map, for example, a horse kicking out in a stable because of the disturbance of rain on the corrugated roofs, thus providing a need here to investigate suitability of materials, costing, budgeting and prioritising; a horse choking on a sweet wrapper will lead the group into looking at ways of alerting the staff and the public to this issue; several horses with damaged hooves may invite the children to design tests to assess the strengths and weaknesses of surfacing materials.

In order to encourage the children to read with care I might introduce the idea of checking horse records (see Appendix III) so that when they are transported we don't get muddled, along the following lines:

"We know some of the volunteers don't read too well so maybe if we just draw in the markings and colours on this, then they can just check the horse against the diagram."

The process of drawing the markings on demands that the children scrutinise the text and copy details exactly. It also serves to build their belief in the existence of the horses. They can use this method to invent their own horse descriptions.

The forms and accident reports have to be authentic. Therefore, the language needs to be true to the world of the stables. When I planned this Mantle of the Expert structure I was constantly thinking of truthful ways in which the children could learn the vocabulary without teacher-telling. By placing a chart for the 'new helpers who don't know all the different parts of the horse yet' in the 'office', children will have a useful source for supporting their own developing understanding and expert vocabulary.

Anything could happen in their stables, depending what you want them to address in the curriculum. You may introduce roles which inject problems for them to deal with. This may be a local farmer whose horses have been attacked and is concerned about the open access we provide at our stables. This will lead

Table 1

Ragwort Yew tree	Poisonous plants and trees
Fields sectioned off Fields with meadow, grass, crops	Implications for resting grass; learning about grass and grazing/effects of crops on the soil
Barbed wire fencing	For the new stables they would need to look at suitable material for fencing and costing of it
Roofs - labelled, corrugated or tiled	They would need to consider the usefulness of these materials
Gravel surfacing	Investigating the effects of different surfaces on horses hooves; various kinds of transport
Electric points Water points	
A main road dividing two fields	This would take you into Health and Safety issues and regulations; also the dangers of horses being fed by the public; signs for the public - types of lettering etc.

the children into the problem of security and of protecting the horses in their care.

This richness of approach allows for the work to develop and grow. Through detailed and thoughtful planning, this system will encourage a deep investment in the work from the children because as experts they will be empowered to run something that will become essentially theirs.

John MacBeath (1997) in a recent article describes a youth's response to his schooling: "Your whole school life is memorise, memorise, memorise, but afterwards you remember nothing." MacBeath argues that "In much of the so-called problem solving in classrooms, it is the teachers who present the problems, and often provide a method for solving them. But the vital step, recognising and defining the problem, is left out." As experts, children will carry the responsibility for recognising and defining problems.

Further information on Mantle of the Expert

A teachers' pack and video entitled 'What's in Store?' details a Mantle of the Expert programme which addresses Drug Education at Key Stage 2. It contains a unique record of the structure devised by Dudley LEA in collaboration with Dorothy Heathcote. It is available at a cost of £35 (£30 to NATD members) from: Publications, Saltwells EDC, Bowling Green Road, Netherton, Dudley, DY2 9LY, telephone - (01384) 813706. The work contained in it is inspired by the recently published text *Drama for Learning*, by Dorothy Heathcote and Gavin Bolton, 1995, Heinemann.

References

MacBeath, J. (1997). 'Unlock the secrets of the thinking brain'. *Times Educational Supplement*, June.

Thorp, and Gallimore (1988), cited in Moll, L.C. (1990). *Vygotsky and Education*. Cambridge University Press: Cambridge.

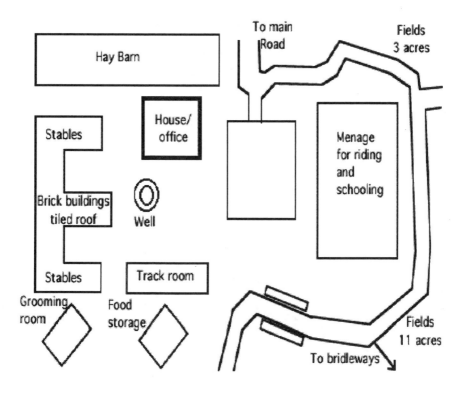

Wellhouse Stables
Accident Report

Date _July 9th._

Name of Horse _Grant._

Name of Rider (if applicable)
Julie Eccles

Details
Horse bucked. Rider a bit inexperienced - pulling too tightly on the bit.

Signature _S.R. Keene_

APPENDIX III

Name	Jack
Markings	Brown and black points
Height	16 h.h.
Age	11 years
Colour	Bay brown
Character	Sensible, docile, willing, hardy

Special Note
Keep him off grass in summer - daytime. Has suffered from laminitis. Watch his weight. Needs regular exercise.

Name	Rising Star
Markings	White spots on dark
Height	12 h.h.
Age	8 years 6 months
Colour	Appaloosa
Character	High spirited, kind temperament

Special Note
Tendency to buck - calmer when put with older mares.

APPENDIX IV

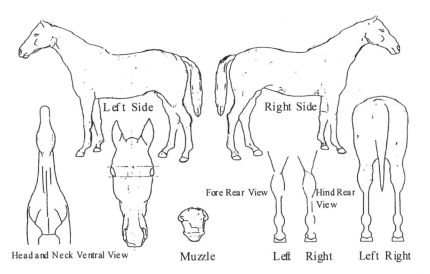

Left Side

Right Side

Fore Rear View

Hind Rear View

Head and Neck Ventral View

Muzzle

Left Right

Left Right

21

Teacher in Role for Beginners

Kate Katiafiasz

Kate Katiafiasz is section leader for Performing Arts at St. Philip's Sixth Form Centre, Birmingham.

We began the workshop by asking, what is the difference between being an actor in role and a teacher in role? To get an idea of how it feels to be in role as a teacher we did one of Bertholt Brecht's exercises in demonstration acting; by imitating somebody who has annoyed us lately, and we noted that the demonstrator:

- refines and selects gestures
- maintains eye contact with audience, and
- can go in and out of role.

So how could this style of acting be of use to the teacher?

Story into drama

With primary children, or year seven or eight who are new to drama, teacher in role can help a teacher slide the class from the safe though passive state of listening to a story, into active participants in a drama. Or, as I tell classes, "at first you will be listening to a story about other people, in another place. But gradually, bit by bit, you will find yourselves getting drawn into the story, so that (and if it gets scary we can stop at any time ...) it will seem as if the story is happening, **now**, to **you** ..."

We then went through a drama lesson based on an idea from Debbie Powers[1]. I will not try to make the lesson come to life on the page, but briefly sketch it for you. Initially the children are listening to a story about a group of school kids, like themselves, who are going on a field trip with a teacher they don't like. Gradually the narration becomes more sensual, to evoke the context in which the children find themselves - on a rainy deserted moor at dusk. To make matters worse, their teacher, who they never trusted, begins to act strangely. At this point the teacher-narrator starts to signify she is going to imitate the teacher in the story; "she walked very slowly, like this ..." (teacher walks slowly), "and seemed to be looking very hard at her map ...", (teacher scrutinizes map) ... "it was soon obvious to the children that they were lost ..."

This use of teacher in role - where the teacher slides in and out of role until the class are comfortable enough with the drama to participate - is called **shadow** role: (for a fuller description see Wagner, 1979). Debbie Powers[1] has elaborated on this model, so that the teacher's voice is in role, while her gestures are those of the narrator, or conversely, her voice could be that of the narrator, while physically her actions demonstrate the role. Eventually, the teacher in role freezes or takes a back seat or exits, to enable the class to claim autonomy: they take decisions as if they were the kids in the story, in *their* predicament.

Using Teacher in Role to slide from story to drama - some exercises

In the workshop we practised these skills in pairs, using the Red Riding Hood story. One partner (*A*) set the scene, narrating a description of the forest using as many of the five senses as seemed appropriate; the other partner (*B*) was to be introduced as the wolf - the narrator gave an attitude, an action, and introduced a few words from the wolf. The forest was conjured up, first as a bright, sunny place full of colour and flowers, next as a dark and sinister, dank-smelling and intimidating place. We realised the symbolic significance of the forest as we went along. The wolf was suave, leaning against a tree looking amused in the first example. He held out his paw to Red Riding Hood, carefully retracting his claws, (*B* gingerly adjusts cuffs, and offers 'paw'), and said ... (*B* says) "well hello"... . It is hard to do this justice in print - the images and roles created were marvellously vivid. In another example the wolf "looked bristly, like an old scrubbing brush, and smelt like dead bodies. He emerged through the hedge casually picking off the bits of straw that were stuck to him (*B* casually picks off imaginary straw from shoulder). When he smiled, (*B* smiles), Red Riding Hood could see pieces of red meat stuck between his teeth (*B* picks teeth noisily and beams)".

There is something magical about simultaneous narration and action which can transform the most respectable teacher into a smelly old wolf - in the mind's eye - of course!

Forum Theatre and Teacher in Role

One progression from the story transformed to drama, could be forum theatre, using teacher in role. Our sensual storytelling had been so successful, that we decided to stay in the forest with the bristly old wolf as he picked his teeth. One brave volunteer was to be Red Riding Hood as she encountered the wolf (teacher still in role), with the 'class' of conference delegates ready to freeze the wolf with a clap and give Red Riding Hood advice if they felt she was in danger. The wolf's aim was to find out as much as possible (without frightening the child), while Red Riding Hood was to 'suss' out the safest way of dealing with the situation - with the help of the class if they felt she needed it. The great advantage of this model for drama, is that the class have started the lesson passively listening to a story, but are now far more in control; they can silence the teacher when they need, to discuss the best ways of dealing with potentially dangerous situations - all in the protected fictional context. And in a strange way, the more vivid the fictional context, the better the metaphor functions for them. With a real class, it may have been necessary to put in a strong constraint to emphasize the danger to the child; a discussion about the size of wolf teeth and claws, perhaps. The more difficult the challenge, the more serious the engagement of the children.

Other types of Teacher in Role

For the remainder of the workshop time, we looked at Norah Morgan and Julianna Saxton's (1987) very useful teacher in role archetypes. We explored how useful the **"helpless"** role can be for a teacher who wants the class to take control, by setting up a scene with a pregnant girl (teacher in role), who has been out all night and will not speak to her anxious and concerned friends (class). I always enjoy the role reversal here - *I* get to be the moody uncommunicative teenager for a change! We also looked at the **absentee role**: a group of anxious astronauts, posing for their last publicity photo try to look fearless in spite of a recent secret briefing about another accident on board their space station. Their colleague, the absentee teacher in role, joins them late and has to be up dated, as they all say 'cheese'.

Other uses of Teacher in Role include: Information Giver; Information Seeker; Devils Advocate; Narrative Role; and Confrontational Role.

References

Wagner, B.J. (1979). *Drama as a Learning Medium.* Hutchinson: London.
Morgan. N. and Saxton, J. (1987*). Teaching Drama: a mind of many wonders.* Heinemann: Portsmouth, New Hampshire.

Notes

1.   Debbie Powers teaches at Golden Hillock School in Birmingham, and from her I have learnt a great deal about Teacher in Role.

Contexts Between Play, Drama, and Learning

Luke Abbott and Brian Edmiston

Luke Abbott is a schools adviser for Essex.
Brain Edmiston is a professor in Drama/Theatre and Education at Ohio State University.

In this workshop we explored some aspects of the contexts between play, drama, and learning[1]. We developed the view that when we use drama in the classroom the context is ideally both playful and dramatic, as well as a space in which learning occurs.

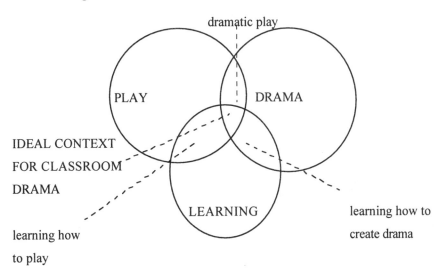

Figure 1   Contexts between play, drama and learning

We developed this diagram (see figure 1) in order to illustrate some of the points we wanted to explore in the workshop. The centre of the diagram is the overlap between play, drama, and learning - the space where we hope to spend most of our time in the classroom as we create with the children the context for our work. In this context, children and teacher are both playing and creating drama; they are also learning about the topic which is being explored in the work.

We illustrated some of the overlaps and differences in the contexts of play, drama, and learning. After asking for examples from participants of what children play on their own, we used one of these and put participants into groups of three. Two played at 'hairdressers' as the third observed and considered why, if they had been observing children at play, they might consider intervention. The open-ended play of the pairs was shaped and given some dramatic form when Luke gathered the players together and asked them to introduce and develop something which the watcher might consider 'controversial'. Now, in addition to imagining the tools and procedures of caring for hair, the players also paid attention to the shape of their interactions, the evolving content, and in addition they added some dramatic surprise. As examples, one person wanted a gang-style haircut while one hairdresser was sharpening a razor like Sweeney Todd. What could have been repetitive safe play had been shaped by drama and a potential learning context was developing - a space where one person trusts another to cut and shape their hair.

We discussed when and why as teachers we should (and should not) intervene and interact with the children. We noted that, as teachers, our decisions about when to intervene and interact with the children are based on our learning objectives in tandem with our observations about the needs of the specific children with whom we are working. In the fictional context we want the children to cooperate and be emotionally safe as they explore the content. We also noted the danger of censoring content - from death to gangs - topics with which we may be uncomfortable yet which children may want to explore.

In the classroom we want children to play as they create drama with or without the teacher otherwise the drama will not be theirs. Drama gives the work a 'body', but in play we discover its 'heart'. Play is imagination in action and play is where caring is born as we imagine from the perspectives of other people - from hairdressers to gang members. Drama which is structured by the teacher as a series of exercises or encounters may appear to an observer to be dramatic. However, unless as the children interact they are actually playing with ideas, feelings, and perspectives which they care about, then the experience for them will be emotionally empty. In addition, when we pay attention to the content of the work - what is being learned - then teacher and children discover the 'head' of the work. When we become clear about our purposes and learning objectives - from cooperation to learning about gangs - then the work has a centre around which ideas and experiences can turn and be considered from different points of view. Most importantly, we can then make informed decisions about when and why we interact with the children.

Contexts
Play contexts
Children will be 'just playing' when they explore ideas on their own terms in a play context when, for example, they replay and expand on events and conversations they have overheard at the hairdressers. The value of play contexts for exploration and socialization are well known. Rather than regard play as something which is not work or not serious, we regard play as an imaginative mode of being and interacting which takes us beyond the space of the actual into the realms of the possible. The hairdressers can become a site for exploring the implications of social resistance or even murder. When we play we experiment

with ideas and metaphorically try out different ways of seeing and interacting in the world. We are playful when we are not literally concerned with survival. When children, for example, are not hungry, tired, angry, or worried about being judged then they will tend to be playful. When we play with children we can create shared fictional worlds which can be shaped by dramatic form and become sites for learning about the world.

Drama contexts

At other times, children may be 'just making drama' in a drama context - concentrating on getting right the theatrical or technical aspects of sharing ideas dramatically. Children who are 'showing' their work to others are often concerned about who stands where as well as who says what and when. Classroom drama ideally occurs in the dramatic play overlap between drama and play - where the free-flowing energy of play is socially shaped and given form through interactions and through the teacher's structuring decisions. For example, in making a film for trainee hairdressers the children could still be concerned with how to show their work, but the form of the work would be intrinsic to their play rather than separated from it as a performance.

Learning contexts

When the children are 'just learning' they won't be engaged in drama - they may be reading, writing, talking, experimenting, or researching with others in a learning context. It is when children are learning at the same time as they are playing and making drama, that the context of the work becomes most powerful and we have the ideal context for classroom drama. Then the talk and image-making with and between the children explores matters of importance both to the children and to us as teachers. When we interact within the fictional world we are able to explore beneath the facts, creating experiential, social, political, historical, cultural, and ethical layers of meaning. (See figure 5 in Brian Edmiston's Keynote address). If the film for trainee hairdressers dealt with how to interact with clients who ask for gang-like haircuts then the work could begin to explore some of the sociocultural and political reasons for gangs and touch on ethical dimensions like client privacy.

Teacher-Children interactions

We identified three categories of teacher-children interactions:
1. to learn how to play (the overlap between play and learning);
2. to learn how to create drama (the overlap between drama and learning);
3. to learn about the content of the work (the overlap between play, drama, and learning).

Learning

How we view 'learning' is critical to our decisions about when and why to intervene and interact with children. A behavioural theory of learning assumes that meaning is given to us and that we learn best through reinforcement and external rewards and punishments; others need repeatedly to tell us how to behave, what to think, and what is 'right.' This view of learning, exemplified by Pavlov's dogs salivating for food in response to the sound of a bell and Skinner's rats scurrying round mazes, is much more pervasive than we might expect. Phrases like 'I can't believe she said that,' 'How many times do I have to tell him?' or 'If you're good you'll get out early,' betray this theory of learning. In the classroom we are behaviourists when we believe that we can teach by telling children what to do or think.

A 'sociocultural' and 'constructivist' view of learning, in contrast, emphasises that we can only teach when children want to learn with us and that understandings are constructed as people interact and dialogue with each other. Though we can tell children information and views, we must build on the children's interests and questions about the world because unless children are self-motivated they will not really listen or enter into meaningful dialogue. Further, meanings are not predetermined but are always created by individuals as they connect their understandings of new experiences with their existing views and understandings. Exemplified by democratic conversations and respectful equitable struggles over competing views of society, this theory of learning leads us to look for social and historical, as well as individual reasons for actions and to promote authentic dialogue among and with children. It is this view of learning which leads us to use drama to set up dialogue among different perspectives without prejudging some as wholly superior, and to say such things as: 'How do you see this?' 'Let's talk about this,' or 'Why do you think she feels that way?' Our decisions about when and why to intervene and interact with children will be based on a view that we need to dialogue about events from many different points of view.

Learning how to play

If children are not playing together productively then we must intervene. If some children are excluding others, for example, boys saying that girls cannot run their barber shop, or if they are destroying the work or using play to be mean, for example, using an imaginary razor to actually frighten another child, then we will not allow the play to continue unchallenged. We can intervene within the play to ask a provocative learning question like 'Is it fair that girls don't get to run the hairdressers?' If necessary we can always talk with children directly about the need for 'the laws of play' (see figure 2) and help them agree on inclusive and fair ground rules which make sense to them.

We can set up conversations among and with the children, both in and out of fictional contexts, so that all can be heard. We also model how the laws of play operate to create spaces which are safe, playful, and open to the respectful sharing of everyone's ideas. Then, within fictional spaces we can together examine both the 'dark' and the 'light' sides of humanity - from murder to heroism.

We noted that teachers sometimes also need to learn more about how to play with children, for example, how to ease in and out of different roles, how to

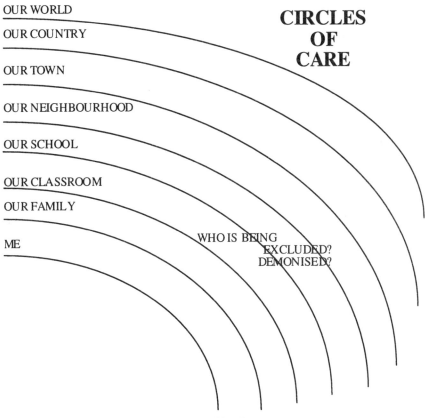

OUR WORLD

OUR COUNTRY

OUR TOWN

OUR NEIGHBOURHOOD

OUR SCHOOL

OUR CLASSROOM

OUR FAMILY

ME

CIRCLES OF CARE

WHO IS BEING EXCLUDED? DEMONISED?

Figure 2　　　　Circles of Care (L. Abbott)

see the world from previously considered perspectives, how to let go of preconceived endpoints, or how to listen to children and create understandings with them about topics of concern to them. We may do so if we stop trying to direct or censor play and concentrate instead on learning more of the possibilities of play. By joining, as an equal player, children's play in homecorners or on the playground around a story like Sweeney Todd, we could discover, for example, what intrigues children about the story.

Learning how to make drama

With younger children we teach about dramatic form mostly indirectly - through creating experiences of the power of drama to shape, sharpen, and deepen the ideas and experiences which are being explored in the work. For example, the dramatic tension of not knowing whether a hairdressing client might be a gang leader in disguise, significantly changes the quality of the interaction.

Sometimes we will want children explicitly to learn about some of the 'laws of drama.' We may talk about the elements of interaction, now time, tension, contrast, mood, imagining perspectives etc. in our reflections on the experiences of a piece of work and then discuss how everyone in the class can harness these dramatic forces to create powerful shared experiences.

As teachers we can also learn from those children who have developed a keen sense of the dramatic. When they come up with ideas or interact in ways which 'fit,' if we can relax enough to play along with them then we may find that the work has been deepened and enriched. For example, a child who enters the hairdressers as a police officer asking for information about suspected gang members has introduced a dramatic tension which would heighten any ethical dilemma about protecting client privacy.

Learning about the content of the work

Ideally, this will be the main reason for our interventions and interactions. As we pay attention to the mood and deepening interests of the children we both facilitate their play and shape it dramatically. But we also pose questions which press and probe for meaning-making as we ask for interpretations, views, and decisions. By focusing the children on the implications for people of their choices and actions within the fictional world, the children will consider aspects of the topic which we think are worth learning about. We will examine examples of these interactions in the following example.

The mining example

To conclude this paper we describe an hour-long episode from the workshop, led by Luke and analyzed by Brian. Analysis will be in italic type.

1. Discussion

We displayed, on an overhead, a photograph which showed a miner on a stretcher, being carried out of a pithead. (For copyright reasons the photograph cannot be reproduced here.)

We used the context diagram (see figure 3) in order to talk about what would be worth learning about mining. Responses included: coping with death; the politics, history and culture of mining; the choices which workers and mine owners had; the social consequences of mining and pit closures; as well as the ethical tension between a need for jobs and a need for safety.

We wanted to show that what is worth learning goes far beyond the facts and, further, that rather than there being a single view on a topic, we can always uncover multiple competing perspectives.

Figure 3   Context diagram

2. Imagining a coal mine

Participants were asked to close their eyes and imagine a coal mine - to wander around it in imagination, to look at the equipment and to call out the sorts of things they were seeing. Participants saw: wheels, cages, darkness, water, buckets, rails, a canary, dirt, a person lying on the floor, etc.

Participants were individually playing with ideas and creating images of coal mines. They drew on whatever knowledge they had of mining which was sparked by our discussion of the photograph.

3. Taking up a perspective

Participants were asked to 'look with the eyes of an inspector of mines' - one who has 'eyes that look for details, for things that could cause problems.' Then, with a partner, they talked about the things they had seen and they were encouraged to ask each other for details.

The participants looked again at the images they had created but now with a critical eye. In asking them to be selective and suggesting a way of looking the teacher was creating a space to move their individual imaginative play toward a shared drama context.

By sharing their images they could clarify for each other and amplify their ideas collectively. They were also developing the beginnings of the shared perspective, or 'frame,' of an 'inspector of mines.'

4. Recording details and considering action

As participants shared, each was asked to jot down the details they had noted. Then they were asked to work together to convert details like 'rust on wheels' into 'issues for action.' Connection was also drawn to their existing views on, and experiences of, inspection when the teacher said to write the issues for action 'like in an OFSTED report.'

The frame of inspector was intensified through hinting at their responsibility for the actions needed to redress the potential problems previously noted. The feelings of inspecting and being inspected were deepened through connecting them to feelings and opinions which had been touched on earlier that day during B. Varley's Keynote address, sub-titled: 'Taking the F out of OFSTED.' Also, those participants who considered possible action were thinking dramatically as they imagined how the present presages the future.

5. Developing the perspectives of inspectors and managers

The group was divided into two halves for only a few minutes. One person from each pair joined the teacher and the others gathered together as inspectors to make their report. The teacher talked to the group who had gathered with him as if they were all mine managers - 'We've had the inspectors in and they're filling out their reports now.' He did not try to create a negative 'conflict' but on the contrary emphasised a non-confrontational and status quo viewpoint that once they had heard the reports it should soon be 'business as usual.' They looked at the inspectors as they deliberated and wondered about what they might say.

The participants' perspective of inspector was deepened in the dialogue about the issues for action as they asked questions of each other about what might happen if action was not taken, and how repairs would have to be made. The managers' perspective was easily adopted since it was simply a shift in point of view and responsibility relative to the details of the mine which they had already created - the managing (rather than inspection) of cages, tunnels, coal removal, etc.

In working to avoid a stereotypical conflict between 'us' and 'them,' and a potential drift into an immoral space where each side defends its position but fails to uncover complexity, the work stayed in an ethical space where different views could be shared and participants could learn through dialogue. Everyone was playing with ideas but within agreed-upon dramatic boundaries which deepened one position without dismissing another.

6. Encounter, in pairs, between perspectives of inspectors and mine managers

The teacher brought the managers to the inspectors and politely thanked them for the inspection - the implication was that they had nothing to hide and nothing to fear. 'Good day. I have brought the mine managers here and we've come to listen with open ears.' He asked how much time the inspectors needed to make their reports and was told five minutes. Then the pairs reconstituted but now they interacted as an inspector presenting and a mine manager reacting. Inspectors were polite and stressed that they were mostly satisfied yet they noted that there were also some troubling safety issues which would have to be addressed. Mine managers responded and tended to downplay the implications for workers.

The teacher mood and attitude continued to work against an escalation of unproductive conflict and instead the social conditions of the need to listen were assumed Dialogues between different views were fostered - the conditions which are necessary for learning, in this case, about working conditions and the need for safety. The pairs could play again though now they would do so from two different perspectives.

7. Public encounter

Within a few minutes the teacher spoke to the whole group and asked the inspectors if they had finished. However, some of the inspectors politely made it clear that safety rules had been broken, that working hours were too long, and that some extensive changes would have to be made. Managers disagreed about the need for any substantial changes since they said that there had never been any serious problems identified in the past. One manager asked the inspectors to clarify: 'What are you saying we need to do?' The teacher asked them to consider the implications of their proposed actions for the mine: 'Are you saying that we need to close the mine down?'

The individual reports of the inspectors were given a public space so that the effect of their proposals could be shared, made more explicit, and the managers could publicly respond to them. The participants continued to play with ideas, but by dramatically repositioning their interactions in a public arena the teacher was asking them to reconsider all that they had previously said and could press them into thinking about some of the learning areas being opened up: the politics of mining, and the choices which mine owners had.

8. Private discussions

Again the groups were separated so that they could talk in private, reflect on their positions, and plan. Each group considered options and wondered what the others might agree to.

Having been asked questions about clarification and possible closure, the inspectors talked about a need to see documentation: time sheets, safety measures, previous accident reports, etc. They talked about what parts of the mine might have to be closed down and for how long. They also pondered on how conditions could be improved and what they might do if the managers refused to cooperate. They considered the consequences of publicity both for the mine and for themselves.

The teacher met with the managers who took up the attitude of justifying the existing conditions. Comments included: 'We've not had serious problems before' and 'It's a question of wages - the workers need to work long hours.' Most managers interpreted the history of the mine positively, others admitted that accidents had happened which might have been avoided. All wondered what the inspectors could and could not insist that they do.

The inspectors and managers both explored responses, from their perspectives, to the questions which had been posed in the public forum. Everyone was engaged in deep dialogue which touched on the social complexities of mining issues including the ethical tension between a need for jobs and a need for safety.

9. Multi-layered sharing

Before the groups gathered together again each looked at each other and wondered about their attitudes. Answers ranged from concern to hostility to being guarded. The teacher then asked each group two questions: 'What can we be open about?' and 'What should we be closed about?' Now participants heard about how both groups would keep certain facts and opinions secret - from a manager 'cover-up' about injuries caused from previous lapses in safety to inspectors dissembling about their lack of enforcement authority. The sharing was intense, measured, and serious.

The drama convention of hearing what would never be spoken in public allowed for a sophisticated multi-layered intermingling of points of view beyond what would happen in playful talk or a standard discussion. The context between play, drama, and learning which had been carefully constructed created a space in which participants could feel and think deeply about the human concerns uncovered in work around coal mining.

33

10. Discussion

The session concluded with a discussion about how the fictional context of nineteenth century mine inspection had not only been about mining but had also illuminated questions for the participants about contemporary school inspections.

Notes

1. We conducted the workshop over 5 hours on Saturday 27th June and over $2\frac{1}{2}$ hours on Sunday 28th June. This article describes most of what happened on the Sunday.

Story into Drama

Paul Kaiserman

Paul Kaiserman is a drama advisory teacher in Leeds.

Aims

The two workshops were constructed to achieve two interrelated aims – to explore the symbolic potential of story, and to attempt to further understand the conference theme by offering an alternative view of the current school curriculum.

I was particularly interested in the use of contrast and contradiction throughout the workshops, by deliberately using an Early Years story as the vehicle by which the workshop members would examine the complex issues underpinning an examination of the role of drama and the arts within the curriculum. This, at times, proved problematic, but it was made overt at the start that we were to be engaged on a journey filled with risk and uncertainty – uncertainty as to outcome, uncertainty as to whether it would work! But this was the second element that I wished to share, that, in order for students to truly share in the learning process, the leader needs to be the lead learner, rather than the lead teacher.

Description – the story

The telling of the story was supported by the use of sounds and movements (each animal, the rain, the thunder) and created by the group. The following is a synopsis, which, in the telling, is clearly expanded:

"In a forest in a far-off land, no rain had fallen for many months. Everything was dying. Animals found shade where they could; the people who lived in the forest stayed in their houses to escape from the merciless heat of the sun.

An old snake painfully slithered across the hard-baked ground. Its skin was black and burnt, its eyes milky-white and blind. In a desperate attempt to find shade, it curled up into a tight ball and buried its head inside the coils of its own body, and there slowly began to die. A voice from deep inside the snake urged it to make one last effort at survival. It lifted its head and called for help.

A rock appeared, thumping across the forest floor. Out of the rock appeared a long twig, which peered down at the snake and asked what it wanted. The snake asked the tortoise (for that is what it was) to help it out of its skin. The tortoise could not, saying that it had only one shell and kept that for the whole of its life, but it offered to call for help.

A tiny spider appeared, and once again, explained that it possessed but one skin. The spider, the tortoise and the snake called once again for help.

A monkey appeared, chattering and shouting, annoyed that it had been disturbed, and demanding to know what all the fuss was about. He too had only one skin that he kept for the whole of his life. The monkey, the spider, the tortoise and the snake all called for help.

A hare, whizzing across the forest floor, screeched to a halt in front of the other animals. He too had but one skin, but, being a wise hare, offered to convene a meeting of all of the animals to decide on what to do. Eventually, after much argument, during which the tortoise thought deeply, but missed every opportunity to speak, the spider was ignored by everyone, and the monkey insisted that all the ideas were his, the hare announced the solution – they would dance for rain. So the tortoise began to beat out a slow rhythm, the spider slid up and down his silken thread, the monkey completely ignored everyone and the hare ran up and down so quickly, no-one saw him.

The people in the forest heard the noise and came out of their houses, carrying anything that made a noise, and everyone danced.

Black clouds appeared on the horizon, eventually covering the sun, and the rain poured down with such force that it cracked open the skin of the snake from the tip of its head to the tip of its tail. From inside the old cracked skin appeared a beautiful new snake – gold, red, blue and green. Everyone was overjoyed. They carried the old snake skin to the tallest tree in the forest, hung it up and danced round and round.

This should be the end of the story but life does not always end happily. Unknown to the animals and the people, hidden by the dense, black rain clouds, the Lightning Monster had arrived. The Lightning Monster was only happy when wreaking destruction, and to see the celebrations going on down below angered him. Finding the silken thread left by the spider, he crept unseen down to the earth, coiled himself up like a spring and shot forth a bolt of lightning that split the tall tree in two. It burst into flames, consuming both the tree and the old snake skin. Everyone froze in horror and fear, and the Lightning Monster, content with his work, climbed up the silken thread and disappeared into the clouds above.

The sun began to shine through, the clouds slowly moving away to the horizon. Just before they disappeared altogether, the Lightning Monster took one last satisfying look at his work – and gasped. For the animals and people, after their first moment of shock, realised that, not only did they now have rain, not only did they now have food, not only had the snake been re-born, but they now had fire – all the ingredients for a huge party, and they ate, danced, sang and played.

The Lightning Monster, at the moment when the last wisps of cloud withdrew from the azure blue sky was heard to say:

Participants were then asked, in small groups, to identify a number of 'key moments' in the story, ones that carried meaning for them. They then attached a symbol to each of these moments – a single word, sound, movement or image, but no attempt was to made to connect them sequentially or in any other way. They were to be treated like mixed-up, disordered pieces of a jig-saw puzzle.

The 'Thesis'

I then offered a short 'thesis' on what could possibly be the position of drama in a new curriculum. The notes for this follow:

- Drama - the usual contexts for its justification include:
  - within English.
  - to support Speaking and Listening.
  - to support imaginative play.
  - to support cross-curricular learning.
  - as an art form in its own right?
  (Ask for suggestions for the list - on a flip-chart.)
- This presentation is a brief overview of thoughts in progress. It's not complete, but may provide some stimulus.
- I'll suggest that all of the above justifications are limited, and in fact don't do drama in particular and the arts in general, sufficient justice.
- I'll begin by looking at world changes, impact on social and political institutions, technological change, the educational system as it currently exists, and as it *will have to evolve*, no matter what political party is in power - all of that in less than an half an hour ...
- Research suggests that whilst population is relatively stable, world structures are stable, *integrated*. During population changes, there is a period of breakdown or *reintegration*. We are in the centre of this now.
- This reintegration can be seen in a number of ways - demand for local, regional power, for example, break up of USSR, former Yugoslavia, Scottish devolution (look what's happened to devolving of power to schools - at least on the surface).
- One very particular aspect is the growth and rate of technological change (though it should be remembered that this does not affect all the world at the same time).
- Population changes over last 100 years. This increase is exponential (see figure 1).
- For instance, the Dutch company who, when they reviewed their current range of electrical and electronic equipment realised that 70% of its products were not even *invented* three years previously.
- Growth of information technology and communication in general which now allows anyone, through the use of the Internet and e-mail,

to talk to anyone, irrespective of position or status.

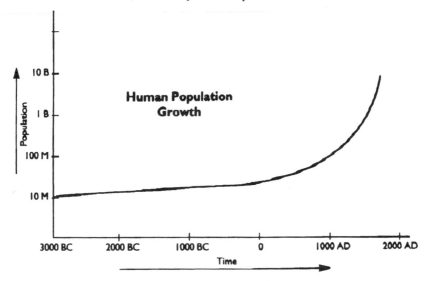

Figure 1 Dr Edgar Mitchell, quoted in '*Creative Teaching and Learning*' (1996)

- With this huge pace of change, it's not always, if ever, possible to know *where* we are going, only that we *are* going somewhere. It's like a stream.
  But I don't want to suggest that we are just in the middle of the stream. Obviously, our education system should provide young people with the ability to swim - to influence where they are going, or at least how they are going to get there.
- The current situation is summed up for me by the recent newspaper story of an 18 year old boy who broke into the Pentagon's system with a £750 computer - and by the way, he failed his A level computer studies exam - but that was okay because he wanted to play the cello professionally anyway!
- So, change is also taking place exponentially and it is easy to ignore its effects until it's almost too late to do anything about it. If we imagine a pond with weed beginning to grow on it from the first day of the month, it would only be by the 27th day that we would realise what is happening:
- The Victorian system of education taught the book. It remained (and perhaps still does) *outside* the stream. It analyses, attempts to predict what will happen next, lists – in other words, it's mainly *cognitive*. But as teachers, we are also in the stream as individuals, and we too don't know where we are going (other than retirement!!). We only know that change is inevitable, its nature, unpredictable.

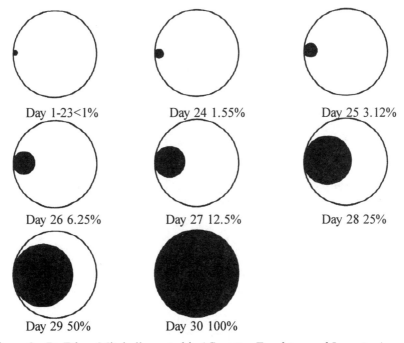

Day 1-23<1%   Day 24 1.55%   Day 25 3.12%

Day 26 6.25%   Day 27 12.5%   Day 28 25%

Day 29 50%   Day 30 100%

Figure 2   Dr Edgar Mitchell, quoted in 'Creative Teaching and Learning'
(1996)

- The qualities that are required to survive, not to drown, are *creative* ones, for example:
    - problem-solving
    - decision-making (alone and in groups)
    - innovation
    - responsiveness
    - confidence in the unknown
    - intuition
    - following an instinct
    - group working skills
    - flexibility.

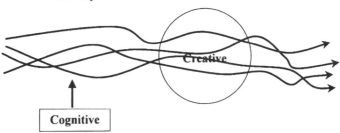

It's these qualities that underpin the process of effective learning in and through the arts in general, and drama in particular.

- So ... if change is a fundamental aspect of the condition in which we find ourselves, and unpredictability is a significant feature of that change, it would seem essential that we provide educational opportunities to practise making forays into the unknown, in supported and non-damaging situations (I'm sure you see where we are heading ...).
- It's no coincidence that employers (c.f.: recent statements by the CBI) are talking about employees who have the *skills to learn* not the skills to work.
- But there is also an *arts context* to this as well, one in which the specific language of drama can be placed.
- It's also, I believe, no coincidence that the arts and young people are now high on a national agenda - for example, the Lottery.
- As educators we cannot provide all of these opportunities alone (nor should we expect ourselves to do so). We need to work in partnership with others - with professionals whose stock in trade is creativity - the actor, the marketing expert, the painter, the engineer, the author, the architect, the scientist, the graphic artist, the product designer ...
- But the key point, and the crux of my argument, is that the issues raised here do not, and *cannot* be confined to the domain of drama and the other expressive arts. The implications for teaching and learning extend across the whole curriculum.
- As drama practitioners, we often recognise the difficulties we encounter in communicating to other colleagues in school the value of our work. Perhaps the time is now right to change the focus of our battle for recognition – to demand, encourage and support, for all teachers, the use of the active teaching and learning strategies which form the vocabulary of drama. The logic of this argument would, therefore, suggest that drama *as a subject* disappears from the curriculum (though this would clearly not be true for the Theatre Arts as a specialist area of study). This approach can already be seen in good primary practice.
- I would suggest that the time is now right to do one of two things:
  - a) wait - in the end the educational system will become so ineffective that politicians will realise that the skills required to be taught lie in the hands of artists, particularly drama teachers;
  - b) send an Exocet - unapologetically shout loud and long about what we do, but by clearly stating that *creative* learning should be part of the core curriculum; that without it our educational system is failing its pupils.

The Story as vehicle

Participants were now asked to return to the moments they had identified in the story, and particularly, the symbols they had created to represent those moments. Taking the issues raised in the 'thesis', together with other thoughts, feelings, doubts and impressions gained throughout the conference, they undertook the task of re-constructing the symbols to make new stories, ones which offered deeper insights into the themes we had been asked to address throughout the weekend.

References

Fryer, M. (1996). *Creative Teaching and Learning*. Chapman.

Cross Curricular Approaches to Drama in the Primary Classroom

Carmel O'Sullivan

Carmel O'Sullivan is a Lecturer in English and Drama, Newman College, Birmingham.

The role of drama in education

Drama is central to the whole education of a child at primary school level. It is now well recognised that learning is a social activity: we learn by exchanging and refining descriptions of our experiences. In all dramatic activities, conversation, argument, interrogation, description and discussion are crucial elements which form a necessary part of the way in which everyone thinks and orders their understanding. Drama enables children to develop the ability to pursue enquiry, and to extend learning and insight. Dorothy Heathcote (McCaslin, 1981) believes that drama functions as a way of making the world simpler and more understandable. The participants can *feel* that it is happening because drama uses the same rules as are to be found in life. She claims that "drama can be a kind of playing at or practice of living" (McCaslin, 1981). Heathcote is concerned with enlarging the frame of reference, developing and binding form and content, and the accumulation of skills and techniques. One of her main purposes is to influence people to reflect, and give consideration to matters of concern. Brian Watkins also emphasises this reflective function of drama in education. He states that the constant always present in drama is the attempt to find some meaning to life. The drama may offer a message for the way life can be lived in the everyday world. Dramatic activity provides an opportunity to distort and refract reality, in an effort to explore every possibility open to us while in the drama. These can then be left in the suspension of the drama or brought with us in our consciousness, to inform our daily lives (Watkins, 1994). Dorothy Heathcote sought throughout her working life to find ways to motivate and empower students in schools. Byron (1988) notes that "She was passionately concerned with the pursuit of knowledge" and that she saw drama as having the capacity to 'humanise schools'. Heathcote believes that part of the role in teaching drama is to help children to consider ideas from different aspects. As a result of this informed consideration, they are better able to resolve problems and issues. She sees drama as a powerful tool for her purposes as an educator. It allows the children to experience, discuss, plan, and reflect on the action. Her philosophy is that by using these different devices, it helps fasten the lesson into meaning. Heathcote speaks about education in a wider context than usual educators do, and she places drama as the tool at its very heart. Wagner (1979) argues that "Whatever the curricular area, she [Heathcote] uses drama to simplify and focus on one particular long enough to illuminate it." Brian

Woolland also contends that to teach drama as a subject area you have to work with other subject areas. It gives greater purpose to both drama and to the areas it is working alongside: "It gives a reason for learning" (Woolland, 1993).

Teaching in many schools never gets beyond telling the pupils about what is to be learned, therefore the knowledge remains the property of the teacher. Quite often children in schools are talked *at*, rather than talked *to*, without being encouraged to offer a verbal response. There is often little significant conversation in which children are involved. Such an approach appears to be almost a travesty of what education should be about. Gavin Bolton (1992) argues that that approach can be reversed in drama. It appears that the process of ownership by the learner can be accelerated and encouraged through the use of drama in the classroom (Hargreaves, 1989). Elizabeth Flory Kelly agrees that drama as a process motivates and accelerates, and deepens the quality of learning (McCaslin, 1981).

Ian Bowater contends that drama can offer "an alternative curriculum" (McCaslin, 1981). It is at odds with the accepted practice of straight line thinking in schools, where answers are either right or wrong. In drama the students are asked to think of possibilities, a method that is almost diametrically opposed to straight line logic. Bowater (1981) affirms drama as being the most radical way of teaching *ever* to hit the curriculum. It places the child at the centre of the learning experience, and allows them to build their own bridges of understanding (McCaslin, 1981).

Harry Broudy's life long conviction is that the quality of general education will be enhanced by an art education. He aphorises the struggle of art education to move from the periphery, to the core of schooling, as a tension between 'nice' and 'necessary'. Art has been regarded by many as a luxury in life, but he is firmly committed to the view that it is a necessity for all. He argues that "In a world such as our children are likely to inhabit, the arts are more than a luxury or refinement: they are necessary to make the truth existentially significant" (Smith, 1992). Margaret Klempay DiBlasio has interpreted Broudy's reasoning as implying that "the study of serious art is seen as endowing individuals with the power to interpret mass culture rather than be unwitting servants of its trends" (Klempay DiBlasio, 1992).

Leading into drama work

Finding the correct '*opener*' or '*lead in*' to drama work with children is very important. Drama does not always have to follow on from a story. The use of '*an other*' is a good way of gently easing pupils into drama work. Anything that takes the attention off the individual and involves them either passively or actively, will avoid children feeling threatened by the situation. They can take on a more active role if and when they feel ready for it.

'*Others*' include: photographs, pictures, objects, tape recorded messages, clues, newspaper headings and reports, puzzles, anecdotes, the use of teacher in role and leading questions; all of which can be used to stimulate quite lively discussions. Creating a profile for a person or object introduced in the '*opener*' can engage children sensitively but directly into the work. It is useful to frame the

43

children in a role when they are first examining the material, whether it is a blanket role and they are all junior detectives looking for clues as they listen to the story or tape, or they may be given more specific roles according to the requirements of the context. Framing the children motivates them to engage meaningfully with the content, and it also gives them enhanced personal status.

Making the drama more meaningful

Both Dorothy Heathcote and Gavin Bolton realised that drama structured as conflict does not get the best out of the drama or the students. They argue that constraints make drama more meaningful. But what are constraints? We live by them everyday. There are constraints in our roles in life, depending on whom you are addressing at any given time, for example, the difference between talking to your employer or your friends. They create tension which allows us to explore the relationship between the characters. Withholding something rather than immediately unfolding it can be more effective. The more delayed the exposure, the more increased the possibility for deeper understanding. Constraints slow down the action and build investment from the students, enabling a more meaningful engagement to take place. Drama is about dwelling in the moment to explore the resonances. However, there can be a danger of over constraining so that your pupils feel immobilised.

An easier induction into role

How can we induct children into role comfortably so that they can *play* the role? Whilst an actor would develop a whole technique, we often make the mistake of saying 'be' villagers. By asking children to just 'be' something or someone, they will go straight to the stereotype or else they may feel embarrassed and fool around. Evoking a second dimension of role will counter this. We use second dimension of role to try and find a dimension of the fictitious role that we can identify with. This is a dimension of role that gives us a way of playing that role. Taking the example of being pirates, without a second dimension, you will get stereotypes - black eye patches, parrots, and a funny speaking voice. Instead, give the children a context and a second dimension, elicit information about what type of people pirates are and what might it have meant to be a pirate historically? Ask questions like 'why were they *forced* into that way of life?' Encourage the pupils to think about what they may have done to be outlawed.

When we are taking on a role or asking others to do it, we need to consider the elements that will enable us to play that role. Some things are more important than others to aid successful role play, for example, a carefully chosen concrete prop is useful but not essential. The dramatic elements include: role, attitude to the role, 2nd dimension, objective, counter objective, constraint, tension, dramatic action, context, meanings, signing, and emotional engagement. One can also build up a role using questioning. This is called 'cumulative witnessing'. Role on the wall can be used to build the role or information can be added in the form of a role spider. This is a useful device as the information is stored on the paper and can be used again in the next lesson.

Emotional engagement

Some emotional engagement is necessary for any real learning to take place. In drama we recreate emotions. In real life, when we react to situations with our emotions, we call them first order emotions. In drama, second order emotions are modelled on first order experiences from real life. It is important that students are prepared that they are working in role or fictionally. Although, we must not protect them *from* emotion: we must protect them *into* emotion so that learning can take place. If the drama structure is not properly set up, it can be dangerous for children to experience first order emotions in a drama context. In educational drama, we avoid pure raw emotion as it serves no purpose here. We must aim for an intellectual response. We are after the state of metaxis, where the participant and spectator are awakened simultaneously. It is important that the students are not totally immersed in the drama, as they need to be objective.

Some subject matter may be painful or controversial and children often suggest these topics because they are genuinely interested in them. It is not a good idea to handle such themes directly. Dorothy Heathcote has devised strategies to counter this. She advises that it is best if the children know the outcome of a drama beforehand so that they can face the pain. Like Brecht, she believes in the philosophy that 'if the pupils know what happens, they will not rush to the end'. Therefore, she starts with the end, and works with the past. She emphasises that the more you distance pupils from the event, the more objective they will be. She works episodically: creating episodes which will bring them closer to the event as questioning spectators and not just unthinking participants. Distancing is the key to helping the pupils be objective. Heathcote's idea of frame distancing would argue that you don't start with the air crash but begin with the black box: 'why did it happen?' Heathcote tells us to slow the moment down and dwell in it: "I talk about task not discussing emotion or feelings. Drama wins not by discussing emotion or feeling, commitment to task will bring emotion, it's all task ... I never use character, I use attitude. Drama is episodic, has episodes. An episode can be long or short; always begin with the end. We know what but we don't know why or where?" (Johnson and O'Neill, 1984).

Games and exercises

The value of games and exercises cannot be overemphasised when beginning work with a new class and particularly when you have limited experience in the dramatic field. Indeed teachers with many years experience still use them as part of their warm-up routines or at various intervals during the day when children's attention (and indeed your own) may be lapsing. They are a great way to revitalise students at any time, adding a sense of *fun* to the classroom, and helping to build a good relationship between the class and the teacher. They can also be used as a motivating introduction to a theme or lesson.

There are many varied games that one can play with children of all ages and while some teachers have been known to constitute the whole drama class with games and exercises only, I would not advise it. Apart from the fact that the educational value of the over use of any one medium is limiting, the children may soon tire of them and the wonderful purpose they serve for stimulating and warming-up would be lost. In the context of the primary classroom, I would suggest that one or two are played at various times during the day, helping to gel a group and release tensions.

1. Listening games:
- imagined sounds - at the airport, on the beach, standing in town, living in Africa, living in the 16th century, etc.
- identifying and describing recorded sounds
- sound stories
- whispering messages
- silly sentences
- identifying voices
- selecting the odd one (sound) out
- what does the music mean?

2. Word games:
- 'The Minister's Cat' ('The minister's cat is a *furry* cat; continue in a round changing the adjective)
- opposites game (black - white; sky - sea; tall - small etc.; played in pairs)
- yes/no game (avoid using the either the word yes or no when your partner asks you a question: 'Is your name Carmel?')
- shopping list ('I went to the shop and bought ...'; continue as a round adding to the list and remembering everything that has already been mentioned)
- put two/three/four words (unrelated) in one sentence
- don't use the word '<u>the</u>' or '<u>and</u>' or '<u>it</u>' in a conversation
- 'Simon Says' (only obey the instruction when the caller uses the phrase 'Simon says')
- 'I spy'
- sentence completion
- what would you do if ...? (you lost your dog/found £50, etc.)
- Charades
- 'Sausage', (one person has to answer 'sausage' to all the questions s/he is asked, without laughing: what is your name? Where do you come from?).

3. Brief encounters:
- look at a picture and describe what you see
- tongue twisters
- my happiest/saddest/most embarrassed moment. It helps if the teacher participates also.

- give a reasonable answer to a ridiculous question or vice versa
- name everything in the room/picture without stopping.

4. Discussions:
- explanations e.g. how to make tea, repair a puncture
- descriptions e.g. character in a bus queue
- reporting e.g. accident on the motor way
- running commentaries e.g. school running race or horse race
- enquiring and informing e.g. detective looking for ...
- information/television presenter
- advertising e.g. devise and perform a jeans or new chocolate bar advertisement
- from different angles e.g. discussing the building of a car park in a residential zone from the residents/builders/city council/business people/conservationists etc. points of view
- talk yourself out of this, e.g. accused of bullying/stealing/no homework done/don't want to go to town with your parent(s)
- 'Twenty Questions' (one person thinks of a place/object/book/tv programme, etc., and the others have an opportunity to ask up to twenty questions in order to discover what the person is thinking of).

5. Body movements:
- 'Walk about trust' (the sighted partner leads the blind one around)
- 'Statues' (when the music stops, freeze as a statue. The leader has to try and make you laugh by making silly noises or faces)
- create a wax museum of characters from a story or poem
- create a still image built around a word or a theme, or suggest the essence of a poem, picture, story in a still image
- mirror your partner's hands or movements
- 'Underneath the Arches' (groups of 6-8 form circles, one breaks the circle and starts to weave in and out followed by those behind, whilst still holding hands)
- 'What's my line?'(mime game, where the others guess your occupation).

6. Simple role play:
- 'Excuse me' (approach a stranger in the street and develop a dialogue from this initial question stimulus)
- 'Chairs and pairs' (at the dentist, hairdresser, bus journey: one person is seated and the other develops a dialogue with them as the provider of the service).

7. Creation and invention:
- 'The all purpose sock' (think of novel ways to use a sock)
- 'Amazimbi' (creating a new language)

- strange news (give groups different pieces of news headlines to try and fit them all together and create a short coherent passage. They can add in up to 5 words of their own in the passage)
- 'Off the Cuff' (each member of the group writes down a word and the words are redistributed. When you get one you immediately start talking about it for 2 minutes and the other person has to guess what it is. Swap roles)
- 'Call my Bluff' (three meanings for an obscure word are given and the opposite team have to guess which meaning is the correct one).

Dramatising stories

This is one of the most comfortable and easiest ways of easing into drama. Work can be confined to the classroom, or a corner of the hall with the class sitting informally around you or alternatively create a story corner in the classroom. This applies more particularly with infant classes. I would be cautious about venturing into the hall too soon, as it can have an unsettling effect on children when they are exposed to a large amount of free space away from the familiar surroundings of the class. Involve yourself in the story and become part of the make-believe. Remember to choose the right time for drama work.

- Direct enactment: Infants are able to do this also but at a less sophisticated level than Juniors.
- Sound stories: using various signals and props to invite the children's contribution at certain points in the story. Particularly suitable for nursery or infant children.
- Using the original story to prompt you in a new direction. For example, in the story of David and Goliath, one could explore other possibilities that may have faced them rather than fighting it out. Or you could look for a modern day parallel. Working with Infants: 'What might have happened if Goldilocks went down the other path in the woods?'
- Chain stories. Each person contributes to the composition of the story. It could be written down, illustrated or repeated orally. With older children, a variation can be played whereby each person has to start the sentence with fortunately or unfortunately.
- Last line stories. Work retrospectively to create a story using the last line as a stimulus. For example, the leader may narrate: 'They all piled out of the train, dragging their bags behind them and collapsed, exhausted and dirty, on the floor'.
- Brotherhoods: the aim is to get the students to pick out the important turning point or the part that mattered most to them in the story, and encourage them to think of other instances like it. For example, when the woman tensely opened the letter and found out the news, reminded me of all the people who open letters from the hospital or their exam results or those who make great discoveries. Use one of these ideas to build a story around. The work could be

put together and recorded on a tape recorder or written in book format, or each group could take responsibility for preparing their section in script form and preparing it for performance.

- Picture stories. Use a picture or photo as a stimulus to start the drama: 'Who are the characters? Where are they? Why are they there?'
- Origins of proverbs.
- Stories created from words (for example, working with Infants, the teacher narrates: 'This word has magical qualities, but it has to be said in a certain way, and those saying it need to be arranged in a particular pattern ...', etc. Or a word can be used to evoke a distant land and time, for example, with Juniors: 'This word was used by the Merengey in the Fifth Quadrant, but hasn't been heard since 2357 when their world was assimilated by the Juncars. It is forbidden to utter it. But the word has been used on a secret sonar message for help that we received yesterday from that world ...', etc.
- Stories built around objects. A story can be built around any odd shaped object and developed into an exciting dramatic adventure, (for example, 'This stone has been found outside the King's Palace. The red streaks are the same colour as those found on the stone necklace worn by the King's abducted brother - the former King ...').

Cross curricular approaches

Drama permeates the whole curriculum, therefore, we need to raise its status within schools so that children and teachers see it as being a major part of their work. Drama activities are invaluable as they can tell teachers much about what the child has learned, what they understand about the world, and what is going on in their lives. As educators we should aim to turn children's natural ability to talk and imagine situations into structuring their own work. Drama is not only a subject but a means of learning, a pedagogy, whose implications reach all aspects of school life. Cross curricular drama activities can help in the carrying out of tasks and also contribute to general intellectual growth, and to personal development. Perhaps the most important reason for using drama as a pedagogical tool is to stimulate motivation and interest in education. We are living in an age of mass media and developing technology where education is forced to compete with many apparently attractive stimulants such as television, videos, computer games, etc.

When planning material for a lesson or scheme of work, I find it helpful to do a flow chart or spider web of the topic (for example, 'The weather'), putting in all areas of the curriculum, and then asking myself why might the weather be important in each one. For example, in Geography: for the growth of the crops. I would then create an outline of a story about a time when the rain didn't come or the sun didn't shine and the crops were in danger of failing. I might use a case study of a fictional character to introduce a personal element, someone the children could relate to, and then introduce a dilemma or problem that threatens that situation: 'a wise farmer from the village predicts the coming of a flood, how does he know? What are the signs in nature? We need to understand how and where it might begin, the destruction likely, and what measures need to be taken in order to save the village'. The main guiding question will often involve several subsidiary themes that open up other curriculum areas, such as history, writing, design and technology, etc.: 'When did it happen last? What was done to stop the destruction? (History) Who do we need to contact for help? (Writing) How can we construct a dam to stop the flood?' (Design and Technology)

The work can grow and develop meaningfully, empowering the children, whilst simultaneously exploring many areas of the curriculum. Using drama as a pedagogy is about freeing the imagination to create a rich scenario, that will resonate many layers of meaning and possibilities. I have indicated some examples of ways of working in drama across the curriculum below.

English
Reading
One of the greatest difficulties in encouraging children to read is motivation, and finding suitable material. The use of a mystery novel, from the Ruth Rendell series for example, can be used to enhance motivation and improve reading skills. The following example can be adapted for use with younger children and a range of texts can be employed, including playscripts and poetry.

Divide the novel into episodes (as in a television series), where there is a moment of dramatic tension or an exposition in each episode. Using the text, prepare the reading materials for the first few sessions, such as a newspaper report documenting the details of a missing person; a riddle scrawled on the pavement outside the missing person's home; a police report detailing the contents of a black refuse sack found in the vicinity, etc. It is useful to have some material prepared but not everything, as the story may take on a life of its own according to the interaction of the students, and different reading materials may be needed that deviate from the mainplot in the novel or play script. Frame the children in a role, such as junior police officers or private detectives, appropriate to the content of the material under exploration. Then, in role as a Police Inspector for example, explain to the children that over the next couple of days/weeks you will be exploring the mystery of a missing person and endeavouring as police officers to solve the mystery. The roles may vary and change during the course of the drama, as certain people may need to be interviewed or particular expertise sought. In each session, introduce written evidence from various sources, such as bus timetables, the coroner's report, witness statements, a police interview of a suspect, etc.; all of which can be drawn from the actual text itself or from supplementary ideas that either you or the children propose to move the drama on. These written documents should be disseminated among the children who work in groups or pairs, or at times as a whole class to examine the material and look for clues, etc. If the source text is too difficult for some or all of the children, it can be re-written in language accessible to various levels of the children in the class. Thus, it is possible to differentiate these drama/reading sessions. After examining new pieces of evidence, a class discussion should allow for a sharing of information and the development of hypotheses and plans of action. A large log or chart of information gathered to date can be mounted on a wall in the classroom and added to during each session, to get an overall picture of the mystery and progress made. Reading materials can be made quite exciting by scrubbing out certain important words (i.e. like a cloze passage) or by browning the paper in an oven to give it an aged appearance (like an old map or note). Genuine documents can be referred to, such as articles of the law, if the children decide to mount a trial scene, for example.

Such a scheme of work could continue for several sessions or weeks depending on the motivation and enthusiasm of the students involved. The students can either read the source text in instalments as the drama proceeds or they may choose to read it at the end of the drama activities, or indeed, the text may only serve as a stimulus for the creation of reading material.

Writing

Creative: this is the most common form of writing that children engage in at primary school level, and usually involves children struggling to pen an essay based around *an adventure title* like: 'My visit to the farm'! The difficulty here is that children are expected to spontaneously create an imaginative story literally out of the thin air. It is very important that some form of dramatic stimulus is given beforehand (and I am not referring to the age-old practice of '*discussing*' the topic as a whole class activity first), so that the children actually have something to create a story around. This stimulus may be the introduction of '*an other*' as indicated earlier, such as a map, a tape recording, a note for help, an unusual stone that has been found by the hay shed on the farm, etc. Anything that will begin to open up a mystery or a problem, where characters emerge and can be developed, will help children to create the framework of an imaginative story. I would suggest that the drama activities are conducted for a session, and perhaps the children write the story in the next session or even at the end of a scheme of work.

Instructional: it is important that the children acquire the characteristic features of this form of writing. Initially, these can be rehearsed orally in a whole class session. With Key Stage One children, for example, we can respond to a letter from Goldilocks (read out at the start of the session) who has broken Baby Bear's chair and asks for our help to mend it or who wants to bake a cake for the Bear family to say sorry for eating their porridge. The instructions can be simply mimed or acted out with young children, and then written on a large sheet of paper as a whole class activity. More demanding scenarios can be created to practise writing out instructions once the children are used to the format. The same character can be developed or a new context created. For example, Postman Pat has e-mailed us! (if you are fortunate enough to have access to such facilities) to tell us that he needs to deliver a letter to Mrs. Brown's house but he cannot find the way. The children could co-create a map of the area on the blackboard or on a large piece of paper, indicating where the roads, river, mountains, houses, etc. are. Mrs. Brown's house is marked in, as is Postman Pat's post office as the starting point. The children could orally practise the best way to get to Mrs. Brown's house, possibly exploring a number of alternatives, where the teacher can add extra drama to the activity by suggesting that there are various problems with going this or that route. The instructions can then be written out in groups or pairs, ready to be e-mailed or posted back to Postman Pat.

With older students at Key Stage Two, similar contexts can be created, based on appropriate material, such as rescues modelled on the '*999*' television series or outer space adventures where instructions are needed to launch an escape vessel from *Babylon 5*. Students can write their instructions in code to motivate other groups in the class to decipher the instructions.

Playscripts: these can prove quite difficult to create with students at Key Stage Two. It is important that students grasp the characteristic features of this form of writing early on, and games can be played to help them practise the use of stage directions, direct speech, the use of names before each person speaks, etc. These can be creatively acted out using a well known television advert for example, where students pop up to orally set the scene, and then different students announce the name of the person about to speak, and others can recite the stage directions or various usages of exclamation marks or dramatic pauses, etc. A useful idea to help students get used to devising dialogue is to give them some stage directions and ask them to write the first four/six sentences of dialogue that might immediately follow: for example, 'The door swung open, and the wind gushed into the dark, dreary abandoned cottage. Loud, heavy footsteps were heard on the creaking stairs. Gavin looked at John, who stood motionless in the bedroom, gripped with fear'. Such a context could be used to develop a drama from. The story could be picked up earlier than this particular episode; indeed the students could be asked to write about what had happened up to this point. New problems and tensions could be introduced, which may give rise to new characters and directions in the development of the plot. The playscript can be devised in stages as the drama unfolds or at the end of the adventure.

Cartoons: these can be created as a development of a playscript, where the storyline is translated in a cartoon format or dramatic activities can be instigated to begin devising a story board and characters. Students will find it easier to create characters when they are engaged in a dramatic context.

Poetry: it can often prove difficult to motivate children to read or write poetry. The use of still image or freeze frame can be employed to make engagement with poetry more stimulating and interactive. Children can be invited, initially as a whole class activity, to create an image of a stanza or section of the poem. These images can be discussed and perhaps brought to life as a living improvisation for a few moments. Characters or events from the poem can be discussed and their profiles created, for example: Where do they live? Who is in their family? What are they doing here in this scene/image created by the poet? What might happen next? The answers to this can be created in another still image or if the answer lies in the poem, it can be represented in an image and discussed again. The aim is to try to unearth the layers of meaning that the poet invested in the poem. Children can write their own additional verses to an existing poem or they can experiment with sounds, words, images, pictures, secret messages, etc. in the form of poetry, all of which are made more meaningful if placed within a fictional or dramatic context.

With the remaining forms of writing, the same creative, imaginative procedure can be undertaken to open up the area for dramatic exploration. Indeed, if a scheme of work is devised, several of these forms can be introduced and practised over a number of weeks, while exploring the same story line. For example, the teacher (framed as an eminent archeologist) can introduce a personal advert that was published anonymously in the local paper, which is offering for sale a rare hieroglyph from the tombs in Egypt. The children (framed as archeologists, interested in the preservation of rare historical objects), are challenged to enquire further into this matter and to undertake to write a formal letter in response to this advert, expressing interest and requesting further details. A reply is received in post card format (written by the teacher), requesting a meeting to discuss the sale. The children return a postcard with instructions of where to meet and how to get there. A request is also made for evidence to authenticate the antiquity. A diary entry (demonstrating the correct format of this text type) is received, describing the discovery of the antiquity, and signed and dated by an eminent archeologist from the beginning of the century. A scheme of work exploring different written text types, can continue in such a manner for as long as the interest is sustained. Other areas of the curriculum can be brought in, such as historical research to authenticate the discovery, or an introduction to the concept of carbon dating as a way of establishing the date of the diary entry. A newspaper article could be written by the students at the end of the drama to tell the story to the public.

Speaking and Listening

These activities transcend all curriculum barriers, but it is possible to devise specific activities that encourage children to communicate more effectively with each other. There are many oral communication games available in published format, but it is fun to incorporate the children's own playground games into lesson time. One of the best ways to encourage children to participate in a discussion is to frame the subject for debate as a mystery or as a problem that needs resolving. With young children, the teacher can act as a devil's advocate, adopting a challenging role and surprising the children. Equally, she may adopt a low status role where she needs the help of the children. It can often help if the teacher narrates a little of the context first, to help establish the mood and to allow students to be eased gently into the drama frame. With older students, debates can be organised (possibly linked to the topic being studied) where various points of view are proposed and challenged; for example, groups of children could adopt the roles of business people, builders, local community leaders, politicians, conservationists, unemployed local people, etc. in a debate about building a sports complex on a green area of a community. The children could be involved in researching their specific perspective and formulating their arguments beforehand. Presenting the debate to another year group or even at a parents' evening can often raise the status of the event for the children, as can videoing it, where such facilities are available. Balloon debates (where characters - possibly from a text being studied - have to justify their position in a sinking balloon, in order to save them from being excluded from the balloon), can encourage greater understanding of the characters in a wider context. The remainder of the class can act as the assessors to decide if their arguments are strong enough or not.

Maths
Dramatic activities can be introduced to help with number work, problem solving, and the acquisition of mathematical concepts, such as weight, volume, area, angles, etc. Motivation is often a key factor in challenging children in maths lessons. Drama can be used to provide a meaningful reason why something needs to be done. For example, why I might need to add up or take away a list of sums on a worksheet. Maths activities can be easily built it into a whole drama scheme and vice versa, for example, where the password to open a locked door involves solving a maths problem or the rescue vehicle cannot go up the mountain with the crane until the angles of the curves on the road are established. With young children, well known stories can be used to help in the acquisition of simple number operations. The most important thing to remember is to keep the pace of the lesson moving so that there is an impetus to solve the problem as quickly as possible, 'so that we can continue with the rescue or the escape'.

Science, Design and Technology
Part of the joy of science is developing the imagination, trying things out, experimenting, creating new formulae, questioning, hypothesising, solving problems. Developing a fictional context can involve much scientific activity, while maintaining the students' interest: for example, building bridges in the jungle to cross wide ravines, testing materials to make a boat to escape from a desert island, inventing ways to protect the national museum which has been rumoured to be under threat of attack from a highly sophisticated gang of thieves, etc. An important point to bear in mind is that the context for the exploration is *possible*, and then let the children exercise their imaginations, building on existing scientific knowledge; which is after all how everything gets invented.

Geography
Geography offers many possibilities for dramatic exploration in terms of both human geography (concerning social issues: poverty, housing, pollution,

54

etc.), and physical geography (concerning rivers, mountains, volcanoes, maps, directions). Volcanoes clearly offer a host of exciting dramatic possibilities, where the factual information can be built into the fictional context. Or environmental issues can be examined where the students are framed as environmental scientists, and are investigating a large multinational company accused of dumping chemicals into the sea. The students would need to acquire a lot of factual information in order to prove their arguments against the highly skilled legal and environmental spokespeople of such a large company. Letters to the company, role play interviews, teacher in role, hot seating, newspaper articles, television debates, etc. could be built into a scheme of work where the children are acquiring the important environmental information and using it in a *potentially* real context.

History

This subject lends itself particularly well to exploration through drama, as history is full of exciting real life events and characters. One of the most important things to examine in history is: *Why* things happened? Could they have been different? In what way? Thus allowing us to learn from the mistakes and positive examples from history.

Using historical data from an era (the Romans or the Aztecs), you could do a case study of a family, establishing their daily routines and responsibilities, and then introduce some tension or dilemma that may have faced someone in *that* position at *that* time. All the factual information that needs to be taught can be built into the episodes of the drama; for example, studying the story of a runaway slave in ancient Egypt, and exploring the dilemmas that s/he may have had to face.

Physical Education and Dance

These disciplines can be made quite stimulating for younger children by introducing dramatic elements into the work. The game 'We're Going on a Bear Hunt' is quite common but other creative stories can be devised which require the children to engage in physically demanding activities. An obstacle course, which can also be conducted in the classroom, involving chairs, bags, tables etc. can be created as a landscape. The lights can be dimmed and the curtains closed to create a particular atmosphere which can be very exciting for children about to embark on an adventure, narrated by the teacher. Constraints can be built into the narration to monitor noise levels or undesirable movement, through indicating that we must remain still or silent at any particular moment or we risk alerting the attention of ... 'the guards at the castle'!

Religious Education and Personal and Social Education

Issues such as the importance of being a good citizen and neighbour; exploring stereotypes (people who live on their own or wear dark, long clothing must be witches is a favourite of young children); how to care for each other; sharing and giving; and the important tenets of all the major world religions, can all be built into a dramatic context and effectively explored through that focus. Children's views can be challenged and developed through creating fictional scenarios where quite difficult decisions have to be made by characters in the drama. Maintaining distance through the use of exploring the lives and decisions of *other* fictional characters, protects the children from personal exposure in classroom environments. They can express and examine their opinions through the safety of speaking for or against a character, and not overtly as themselves. This is particularly important when working on sensitive issues such as bullying or racism.

Other art forms

The various arts forms of music, dance, the visual arts and drama, can be used with aspects of technology to create an imaginative devised performance. This will involve the children selecting an area of interest that stimulates them. It may be a fantasy theme or a social issue. Simple objects and materials can be used as stimuli in workshops; for example, inviting the children to '*play*' with chairs to see how many different ways there are to interact with them, can create an interesting ritual. Passing bits of paper to each other in different ways, using gestures and movement, can suggest evocative message to an audience. Pieces of material draped along the floor can encourage all sorts of interaction to create images or patterns of movement creating its own meaning. These can be accompanied by music, which may be live if desired (most simply achieved by experimenting with rhymes and chants to create different effects). Various pieces of art that link in with the theme could be used to decorate costumes or the performing space. Appropriate images from a slide projector or video could be projected on to a backdrop. These could accompany 'live' still images created by the children, who could use a beat or dance tempo to 'move into' the image, hold it, and then 'move out' of the image, possibly into another one in a different space. Children are surprisingly adept at creating amazing still images when they are used to handling the form. A note should be taken of the work produced during and/or after the workshopping process in order to remind you and the children of the work produced in each session. A collaborative decision can be taken on how best to incorporate the devised material into a performance. Original or published poems and stories may be incorporated into the production, and presented in a creative way, for example, using a microphone to create an effect; underplaying the recitation with music; presenting a poem in choral form; or involving ritual, where children are placed on different levels in darkness with lamps under their faces, for example. Children themselves are excellent at coming up with creative ways of doing things.

References

Bolton, G. (1992). *New Perspectives on Classroom Drama*. London: Simon & Shuster.

Byron, K. (1988). The Heathcote Legacy. *2D* Vol. 8, No. 1, Autumn.

Hargreaves, D. (ed.) (1989). *Children and the Arts*. Open University Press.

Johnson, L. and O'Neill, C. (eds.) (1984). *Dorothy Heathcote - Collected Writings on Education and Drama*. London: Hutchinson.

Klempay DiBlasio, M. (19920. 'The Road from Nice to Necessary: Broudy's Rationale for Art Education'. Special issue of the *Journal of Aesthetic Education*: Essays in honour of Harry S. Broudy. Vol. 26, No. 4 Winter.

McCaslin, N. (1981). *Children and Drama*. Second edition, London: Longman Inc.

Smith, R. A. (1992). 'On the Third Realm - Credibility and Commitment: In Praise of Harry S. Broudy'. Special issue of the *Journal of Aesthetic Education*: Essays in honour of Harry S. Broudy. Vol. 26, No. 4 Winter.

Wagner, B. J. (1976). *'Drama as a Learning Medium', Dorothy Heathcote*. London: Hutchinson.

Watkins, B. (1994). 'The Social Origins of Theatre'. Unpublished, UCE.

Woolland, B. (1993). *The Teaching of Drama in the Primary School*. London: Longmans.

Reaching Out: Ethical Spaces and Drama

Brian Edmiston

Brian Edmiston is a Professor in Drama/Theatre and Education at Ohio State University.

I asked a colleague, who is very experienced in giving addresses to conferences, for advice about what to be sure to include - 'Begin with a joke,' he stressed. So, here is my joke. A Jewish person who was visiting Northern Ireland was stopped on a back street in Belfast and asked by a sour-faced man, 'Are you a Protestant or a Catholic?' Undaunted, he responded with a smile, 'I'm Jewish.' The man paused for a moment, narrowed his eyes and asked, 'Are you a Protestant Jew or a Catholic Jew?'

I envision this talk as a tree reaching out to all listeners whether you regard yourself as Protestant, Catholic, Jewish, or whatever. The trunk of the tree is my main topic: Ethical Spaces and Drama; the leaves are the practical examples I will give. The roots of this talk lie in my theoretical views of the classroom, learning, the self, and how we view others. Though I will not use these four roots to organise the talk, I will make references to them throughout.

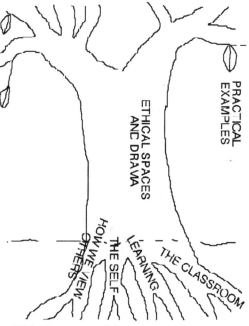

Figure 1   Ethical spaces and drama

I am going to talk about the ideal classroom which nurtures 'ethical spaces' and contrast these with other types of classrooms which create 'immoral spaces' or 'amoral spaces.' I use the terms 'ethical' and 'moral' interchangeably, not to refer to the following of predetermined moral rules, but on the contrary to refer to social spaces in which students and teachers may each encounter, examine, and recreate their unique ethical stances in the world.

Ethical Spaces

What metaphors would you use to describe the ideal classroom? An artist's studio? A mountaineering team? An archaeological dig? How about a family? That is the metaphor Tracey Bigler-McCarthy actually uses in conversations with the six- and seven-year-old children in her combined age classroom[1]. In her classroom Tracey strives to create ethical spaces where discovering how to share and resolve disputes amicably is integral to the children's learning She would agree with Nel Noddings (1984), who argues that 'caring' is 'our basic reality' and that teachers ought to promote the formation of an 'ethical self' which is 'born of the fundamental recognition of relatedness; that which connects me naturally to the other, reconnects me through the other to myself.' Respect is the '4th R' in her classroom. The children learn about the ethics of caring from their first days with her; together they agree on how to convert the principle of mutual respect into their classroom expectations. Along with the children who are in their second year in the classroom, she models how they work together, think about the consequences of their actions for others, resolve problems through listening, create the sort of ideal family they want, and learn that love is at the core of their community. They are all learning to be ethical because, as Peter Singer (1991) says, 'Anyone who thinks about what he or she ought to do is, consciously or unconsciously, involved in ethics.' Their classroom community does not split into opposing sides as they think about how to act over issues like teasing or hurt feelings. Rather, Tracey assumes that they are all on the same 'side' of principles which guide how we 'ought' to act and lie at the heart of their interactions: principles like sharing, concern, decency, equity, and fairness.

Daily life in Tracey's classroom pivots on a fulcrum of empathy. It is assumed that children should try to see the world within and beyond the classroom from other people's points of view as well as their own. However, an ethic of care connects the world beyond school to the life of the classroom. As Tracey says, 'Why should we expect children to care about people in places like the rainforest if they haven't learned to care for each other?'

In drama contexts, the children learned what it means to reach out and care for each other in more challenging circumstances than they would ever hopefully have to encounter in daily life. For example, people placed their own lives in danger as they worked together to rescue their fellow aircraft designers from an aircraft in danger of exploding. They also all gathered together to hold hands, bury the dead, and care for their families. The circles of care which had been nurtured over time were, in fictional contexts, extended beyond their immediate

59

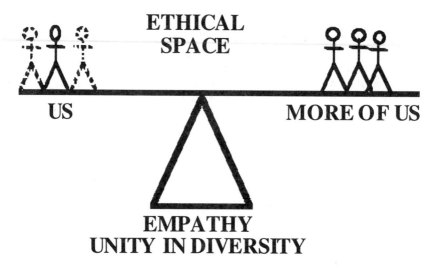

ETHICAL SPACE

US

MORE OF US

EMPATHY
UNITY IN DIVERSITY

What side are you on?
    - decency
    - fairness
    - democracy

What are you prepared to do about it?
    - dialogue
    - struggle

With you
With myself

Figure 2   Ethical space

group. When they designed aircraft they took care to avoid damaging the trees through which they needed to land. When they were lost in the Amazonian rainforest they wondered how native people would treat them and how they should interact with them.

The theme of this conference, 'A Head Taller,' is for me an ethical image of drama's potential to create contexts in which morally, in Vygotsky's (1978) words, 'it is as if a child is a head taller than himself.' One of drama's largely unrealised potentials is fostering the ethical self - the wise self which reaches out, connects us to others, and gives us moral guidance for our actions.

Immoral Spaces

The social spaces of schools and other cultural institutions are not automatically ethical - a morality of care has to be nurtured and created by everyone in a community out of a spirit of good-will. Having grown up in the splintered community of Northern Ireland I know only too well about the destruction of tentative ethical spaces and how easily 'immoral spaces' can be created out of a spirit of ill-will. In a society where nearly all people position themselves and others - even Jews - as on either the Protestant or the Catholic 'side,' people tend to see that 'our' views are balanced against 'their' views on a fulcrum of irreconcilable differences. The hatred which creates polarised positions can easily descend into dismissal and then demonization of the different religious, social, and cultural views and actions of those 'others' who are 'not us.'

When anarchic circumstances are allowed to petrify such hateful attitudes, then ears, hearts, and fists shut tight as yelling and even killing consumes mobs of self-righteous or vengeful people intent on proclaiming their selfhood in acts of monstrous and inhuman destruction. The pictures of the funerals following the recent murder of two police officers in Lurgan leave me asking what teachers in classrooms can do to understand the causes and circumstances of such inhumanity.

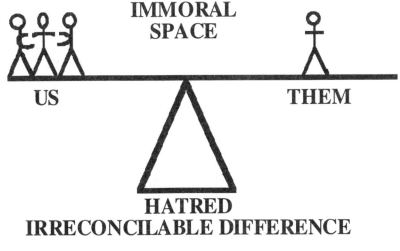

What side are you on?
-ours
-not ours
-fascism

What are you prepared to do about it?
-yell
-kill

Figure 3   Immoral space

Lest we demonize the demonizers, Daniel Goldhagen (1996) reminds us that it was 'ordinary' Germans who enacted the Holocaust and became 'Hitler's willing executioners.' Fascism, hatred, and butchery are not Irish, German, or Bosnian phenomena. Their roots lie in all societies. Given particular historical, sociocultural, and political contexts, the racist divisions which feed genocide can tragically split any society where fascism is culturally bred, socially condoned, and officially supported. Given the pervasive face of evil, I begin to wonder how the contexts we create in classrooms with children may interconnect with the creation or rejection of such inhumanity.

No classroom teacher that I have ever known would support hateful ideals or condone racism. Yet, when we inadvertently promote 'us against them' attitudes, or allow the treatment of other people as objects to go unchallenged, then I believe we fertilize the roots of intolerance - divisive roots which support the growth of spaces of immorality. Instead, I believe, we must promote a spirit of good-will, tolerance, and celebration of difference.

Seamus Heaney (1995), in his Nobel Prize acceptance speech said that poets are 'hunters and gatherers of values.' I think teachers are too. We are 'hunters' of values at times when we seek out ethical dilemmas, take moral stands, and clarify our values. Yet we are also 'gatherers' of values in the day-to-day classroom interactions which always have ethical dimensions.

Another teacher, Mary McCarthy, recently realised the ethical significance of an apparently inconsequential action on her part. A child picked up a penny from the floor, and asked Mary what to do with it. Usually she kept lost items safe and would spend unclaimed money on class treats. On this occasion, however, without thinking she light heartedly said 'Finders keepers; losers weepers' and the child pocketed the penny. It was only after later reflection on the ethical dimensions of this action and the effect on any silent child witnesses that she recognized the modelling affect of an action like this and the potential damage to the ethic of care which she was working to promote in her classroom.

In contrast, the ethical dimensions of small actions can suddenly become apparent, especially in drama contexts. Mary recognised this when the children in her class insisted that the name of their fictional air travel company - 'Safe Travel' - would have to be altered. They had realised that despite their safety measures they could still crash and agreed that customers would be misled by the name. Their ethical decision to change the name might seem insignificant, yet it was one of the many moral gestures in the gathering of values like honesty and decency which not only guided their travel company enterprise but were also principles by which the children had begun to live.

Amoral Spaces

Some teachers believe that rather than deal with honest questions from children about such worrying issues as war, hatred, or death, it is better to shield them from such concerns. They regard children as too young or too vulnerable to think about, or even ask, questions which from an adult point of view they consider too troubling.

Such teachers create what I call an 'amoral space' in their classrooms. There is a superficial 'unity' about the classroom where differences are minimized and the 'sides' to issues remain unbalanced and unexamined in any depth. There may be apparent intense 'intellectual' activity but the classroom is also characterised by an emotional detachment from issues in and out of the classroom.

I was recently in a reception classroom which was bright and filled with children's work. However, there was a uniformity to the work which was clearly guided by a well-meaning adult hand. Against one wall were trays of seeds with an unanswered question written by an adult on a now faded note 'How high do you think the seeds will grow?' One boy left his teacher-assigned work to join me by the trays which had been labelled by the teacher. 'Did you plant all the seeds in your tray?' I asked him. He gave me a look as if I had asked him if he were the Head teacher. 'Naw,' he responded, 'Miss Greenley did.' I looked across to the teacher's desk where Miss Greenley, cool and detached, was monitoring the children's behaviour. The boy caught her eye and returned to his assigned table. Clearly, talking about seeds was not appropriate at that moment. But more worrying, though plants grew at the back of the room the children were not wondering together about them, asking significant questions, or connecting plants to their lives. The children were certainly not asking social questions about the medical uses of plants or ethical questions about the death of plants as food.

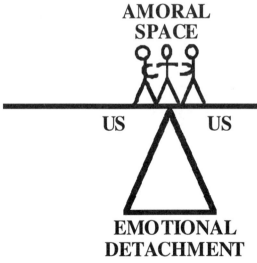

AMORAL SPACE

US **US**

EMOTIONAL DETACHMENT

What side are you on?
   - there are no sides

What are you prepared to do about it?
   - don't ask such questions

Figure 4   Amoral space

'Learning' in this classroom seemed almost entirely factual and assumed to happen as a result of a series of teacher-directed activities. The values which were hunted and gathered in this classroom were teacher-centred and over-protective. This teacher did not seem to understand the critical need for meaningful dialogue about content and the necessity of constructing relational understandings between children's authentic questions, their prior knowledge, and the many different perspectives they could adopt about any topic. Nor was there any evidence that the teacher considered a layered approach to content which would value and open up the sociocultural and ethical dimensions of topics.

Teacher responsibilities

If we accept the ideal of the classroom as a space which is ethical, rather than immoral or amoral, then what are our responsibilities as teachers? Robert Fried (1995) has argued that, 'Students need us, not because we have all the answers, but because we can help them discover the right questions.' Regardless of the content of classroom inquiries, if we look beneath the facts we will discover questions which are worth pursuing with students of any age - questions which will not only lead to new understandings but also to deeper questions beyond the ones we might initially think were the 'right' ones. And at the core of all contexts we can discover ethical questions - questions about the choices which face people and questions about how we would act if we were in similar positions.

CONTEXTS ARE.............

factual	" What did they do?"
experimental	" How did they feel?"
social	" How did they interact?"
political	" Who had power and authority?"
historical	'How was it different in that time?"
cultural	" What shared views did they have?"
ethical	" What choices did they have?"

TYPES OF QUESTIONS TO ASK

Figure 5   Layers of context

An amoral space begins to form in the classroom when students become emotionally detached and do not ask questions which show an empathy with others' situations and points of view. An immoral space begins to form when students do not question their own positions, begin to blame or objectify others, and start to regard themselves as morally superior.

We can move toward an ethical space by creating fictional experiences with students in which they may begin to see others as people who are different but also very similar to themselves. Other people will be seen as having more or less power, social status, or opportunities, yet from an ethical stance it is critical that they are seen as human beings. Further, other people must be seen as enmeshed in social relationships and practices which tend to both promote and resist the creation of ethical and unethical stances. In the classroom we can become hunters of values as we uncover ethical dilemmas which faced those people, present the students with some of their difficult and limited choices, and discover how we might have acted.

When I worked with some thirteen-year-old boys who were researching the Mafia and Al Capone, they seemed to be wavering between an amoral and an immoral position[2]. They could not understand how anyone could have been caught up in the mob to the extent that they would have become killers who had willingly taken part in the St. Valentine's Day massacre. They also said that they would never have joined the Mafia and their dismissive tone implied that anyone who did so must have been morally weak. As Noah said, 'It doesn't make sense. I think they just made themselves all this trouble.'

I asked the boys if they wanted to think about these questions by imagining that they were people who lived at the time of Al Capone. They were eager to act out the shootings and showed me a superficial tableau of the massacre. Then I asked them to imagine that they were recent immigrants to the United States in the 1920's selling something on the street - they decided on fruit from a cart. I entered, turned over their cart, feigned apologies, and said that what they needed was 'protection'. Within minutes they were running a fruit and vegetable shop and as part of their rent agreed to some 'things' being stored in the basement. When I arrived as the police wanting explanations about the illegal alcohol found on the premises and later as a mobster, wanting to know what they had said to the cops and whether or not they still deserved protection, the boys realised that they were caught between the law and their loyalty to their new 'family' - what Pat, one boy, recognised as a 'family of hate.' They reluctantly chose to accept more protection, fake identities, and 'promotion' running a larger store. When they tried to refuse to be 'in' on the next job, on St. Valentine's Day, they found themselves in another ethical dilemma - risk the lives of their families or pick up a machine gun and join the mob. Again, they enacted and showed a tableau of the massacre but this time the people in the Mafia were portrayed with sensitivity and they no longer saw themselves as morally superior. An ethical space had been created with the boys in which many questions had been raised including questions which none of us had anticipated. The 'trouble' the Mafia members were in was no longer simplistically seen as solely of their own making rather their choices were seen as embedded in more complex sociocultural dimensions. As Chris said, 'How could I have thought that it would be easy?'[3] The boys returned to their research ready to explore some of the previously unconsidered experiential, social, political, historical, cultural, and ethical dimensions of their topic.

Vygotsky (1978) realised that 'What a child can do with assistance today she will be able to do by herself tomorrow ... the only good learning is in advance of development.' In working with these boys, I was able to assist them to learn things they seemed incapable of learning alone. In particular, they began to ask and explore more challenging questions. Further, we created contexts in which the boys' experiences began to transcend an 'us against them' mentality so that instead they began to balance the views of 'us' against those of 'more of us.' In other words, though we all morally disagreed with the actions of people caught up in the Mafia in the 1920's, the boys had not dismissed the mobsters' humanity but were trying to understand why they may have acted in the ways they did.

The Ethical Self

In drama we can shape facets of an ethical self. In drama, students can discover new voices and points of view they had not previously considered. These different views are critical, not only for understanding other times or places, but also for shaping the ethical dimensions of the self. Bakhtin (Morson and Emerson, 1990) views the self as a 'conversation, often a struggle, of discrepant voices with each other' and drama can enliven and problematize that conversation which is highly ethical when we contextualise our empathetic struggles over how we ought to act toward others in particular situations - actual or fictional. I believe that we owe it to the children in our care to assist them as they explore questions and 'voices' they discover are important to them. It is also our responsibility to help children to ask more difficult questions and pay attention to the voices of people whom they may have only superficially considered.

Recently, some eleven-year-old children in Molly Hinkle's classroom, encountered 'voices' of race, class, and gender as they struggled with how they would have acted at the time of the Titanic disaster. They became fascinated with moments of separation and represented them in drawings like this one (see Figure 6). The students became obsessed with the intermingling of death, despair, bravery, and hope. Some of the 'discrepant conversations' the children had were in response to questions like these: What do you say when you say good-bye for the last time? Who will you put in the lifeboats? Who will you leave behind? Why are there no people of colour on board? Should women and children go first? Why did most of the poor people drown? Who will the owners reach out to? What was your recurring nightmare? What kept you going?

Dorothy Heathcote (Johnson and O'Neill, 1984) has stressed that it is in dealing with the 'messes' we are in that we are changed 'because of what we must face in dealing with those challenges. 'The ethical spaces we create in our

66

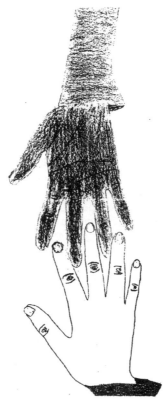

Figure 6   Hands from the Titanic

classrooms are paradoxically the very spaces in which, through drama, we can encounter, and deal with, not only the joys of our humanity, but also the horrors of our inhumanity. In drama, our ethical self can be burnished and transformed in the empathetic fires of the depths as well as the heights of our humanity.

When we face trials in fictional contexts within the classroom we can discover that we may face them together. The image of hands reaching out across time, space, and cultures is for me an image of the ethical self which touches others. It reminds me of more of Seamus Heaney's words from his Nobel Prize acceptance speech when he recounted a dark moment in the recent history of inhumanity. In 1976 a minibus full of Ulster workers was stopped by a gang of men with guns in their hands and hatred in their hearts. The workers were made to line up beside the bus. A gun was waved in front of them: 'Any Catholics among you step out here.' The lone Catholic man did not move when his hand was gripped by his fellow Protestant worker in a signal that said we are in hell, but we are here together. The story does not have a just ending. After hesitating, he stepped forward, only to see all his friends butchered by the masked executioners.

Yet Heaney finds hope in his belief that 'the birth of the future we desire is surely in the contraction which that terrified Catholic felt on the roadside when another hand gripped his hand'. Like the caring hands on the Titanic, the image of hands reaching out across a chasm sustains a moral imperative which cannot be overpowered despite any surrounding horror: my actions are connected with the fate of other people.

Peter Senge (1990) believes that 'Real learning gets to the heart of what it means to be human.' The power to hate and kill is as much at the heart of our humanity as is the power to love and nurture. I believe that authentic education has an ethical dimension which necessitates that children explore the full gamut of our human potential and try to understand what it is that motivates people to do evil as well as good deeds. Senge (1990) continues: 'Through learning we recreate ourselves. Through learning we become able to do something we never were able to do. Through learning we reperceive the world and our relationship to it. Through learning we extend our capacity to create, to be part of the generative process of life.' This could be a description of the education of a strong ethical self.

Seamus Heaney concluded his Nobel speech by talking of the power of poetry. He could equally be talking of the potential power of drama to nurture our ethical selves as he celebrates, 'the power to persuade that vulnerable part of our consciousness of its rightness in spite of the evidence of wrongness all around it, the power to remind us that we are hunters and gatherers of values, that our very solitudes and distresses are creditable, in so far as they too are an earnest of our veritable human being.'

References

Fried, R. (1995). *The Passionate Teacher*. Boston: Beacon Press.
Goldhagen, D. (1996). *Hitler's Willing Executioners: Ordinary Germans and the Holocaust*. Cambridge, MA: Harvard University Press.
Heaney, S. (1995). *Crediting Poetry*. New York: Farrar Strauss Giroux.
Johnson, L. & O'Neill, C. (Eds.). (1984). *Dorothy Heathcote: Collected Writings on Education and Drama*. London: Hutchinson.
Morson, G.S. & Emerson, C. (1990). *Mikhail Bakhtin: Creation of a Prosaics*. Stanford, CA: Stanford University Press.
Noddings, N. (1984). *Caring*. Berkeley, CA: University of California Press.
Senge, P. (1990). *The Fifth Dimension*. New York: Doubleday/Currency.
Singer, P. (1991). *A Companion to Ethics*. Blackwell Reference.
Vygotsky, L.S. (1978). *Mind in Society*. Cambridge, MA: Harvard University Press.

Notes

1. With the exception of the reception teacher whose name is a pseudonym and who works in Essex, I have used teachers' actual names and described classrooms in central Ohio, USA.
2. The classroom teacher was Jeffrey Wilhelm and the classroom was in rural Wisconsin, USA. The students' names are pseudonyms. For more details, see Wilheim, J. & Edmiston, B. (in press). *Imagining to Learn: Inquiry, Ethics and integration through Drama.* Portsmouth, NH: Heinemann.
3. This comment was made in another context following the work on the Holocaust.

The *Full* Range of Culture?

Jonothan Neelands

Jonothan Neelands is a senior lecturer at the Unit for Research in Education, Cultures and the Arts; Institute of Education, University of Warwick.

I want to begin by thanking Dorothy Heathcote (the first speaker of the evening). Over the last few years, I have been asked what my doctoral thesis is about. I have stuttered and mumbled in response. Even now that it is finished I have found it difficult to explain to others. Last week Dorothy did a great kindness by responding at length to the manuscript for a new book that I am writing with Warwick Dobson, Tony Goode and Jim Clarke called *Lessons for the Living.* In her response Dorothy suggested that what we were doing was helping teachers and their students to:

" *... explore human behaviours and experiences in social circumstances ... under fictional pressure"*

This seems to me to be the most accurate description of our work and of our intent.

As you may know the Executive Committee have been working on a new policy document that will be brought before you for your consideration. I want to begin this evening by reading from the introduction to this draft document:

"The function of an educational system is (or should be) to give all young people access to the full range of human culture. (Culture is seen here as the total of current and developing gains in human understanding and practice - in the arts, in the sciences - physical and social, in technology, in philosophy, etc. It is the totality of what humanity, the major learning species, has learnt to know and to do.) Young people need to inherit that culture from those who precede them ... "

I want to reflect on the terms used. In particular I want to stress the need to differentiate between what is 'natural' i.e. immortal and unchangeable and what is 'cultural' i.e. local and transformable. I want to stress the importance of not confusing the two; the danger of 'naturalising' for children what are in fact particular cultural conceptions of living. I want to make this emphasis because it is a critical issue in education; together with families we as teachers have a critical role to play in the socialisation of children. I also want to make this emphasis because I believe the theatre is the art form that humankind has invented to comment on and represent the conflicts between nature and culture.

We have to beware of using the word '**culture**' as a singular term; of suggesting that there is a unified 'natural' culture which is shared by all and which all have access to. To do so is to further reinforce a particular and dominant conception of culture that disregards local differences and identities. By accepting and naturalising the singular term culture we are in danger of further reinforcing the use of 'culture' as a means of creating and reproducing social distinctions. We naturalise the dominance of the refined and restricted culture of one social group at the expense of recognising the complex histories of power and opposition within our society. As Bourdieu (1974) reminds us:

"Schooling serves to reinforce rather than diminish, social differences. The culture it transmits is largely that of the dominant classes ... cultural capital thus participates in the process of domination by legitimising certain practices as 'naturally' superior to others and by making these practices seem superior even to those who do not participate, who are thus led through a negative process of inculcation, to see their own practices as inferior and to exclude themselves from legitimate practice."

The alternative to institutional use of 'culture' as a tool of oppression is to use it, as Bourdieu (1997) also suggests, as 'an instrument of freedom that presupposes freedom'.

It is more appropriate for us, I think, to consider **culture as a field** in which competing collective identities and cultural positions jostle for dominance and to collect the cultural capital that like economic capital provides access to power. Within the field of cultural production we should be working towards an active collective solidarity between cultural positions and traditions that are marginalised or suppressed by the dominant position. A collective solidarity that is based on respect for collective identities within the field of cultural production. As Nancy Fraser (1986) suggests:

"It is the sort of ethic which is attuned to the contestatory activities of social movements struggling to forge narrative resources and vocabularies adequate to the expression of their self-interpreted needs. It is attuned also to collective struggles to deconstruct the narrative forms and vocabularies of dominant groups and collectivities so as to show these as partial rather than genuinely shared and as incapable of giving choice to the needs and hopes of subordinated groups."

We should also recognise that for all of us, and particularly for children, culture is an intensely **local and physical experience.** Bourdieu (1977) uses the term 'habitus' to describe the localised forces of 'hidden persuasion' that shape our cultural identities. In learning language and in moving through the processes of schooling children are moulded into habitual ways of seeing and engaging with the world that are remarkably specific to their local social circumstances (habitat), and as Bourdieu's (1977) definition suggests, this moulding is focused on the body and on learning to consider as 'natural' or 'unnatural' that which is in fact cultural. The dispositions that constitute the 'habitus' are inculcated, structured, durable, generative and transposable. They are acquired through a gradual process of inculcation in which early childhood experiences are particularly important. Through a myriad of mundane processes of training and learning such as those involved in the training of table manners, the individual acquires a set of dispositions which literally mould the body and become second nature.

The body is in many ways the **hinge** between nature and culture. Consider what is learnt through language such as: 'sit up straight', 'don't eat with your hands', 'keep your mouth closed when you eat'. Consider the way in which we naturalise cultural behaviours through the metaphors of 'filthy' and 'dirty': 'Don't touch yourself you dirty little boy,' 'Stop that - it's a filthy habit'. And of course school provides a second authorised culture for children to learn to accommodate themselves to: 'You're not at home now you know, your mother may let you do that but I won't have it in my classroom'. The dispositions that constitute an individual's 'habitus' unavoidably reflect the social conditions within which they were acquired. The Filipino theatre worker, Beng Santos-Cabanon (1995) offers a definition of culture that foregrounds this local experience of culture:

> "Culture is who we are and who we are becoming. It is the food we put on the table, the way we cook it, the utensils in which we eat it, the relations between the people who sit at the table and the people who cook and serve, what is done with the leftovers, what is discussed during the meal, what music, dancing, poetry or theatre accompany it, and the social and spiritual values of those present - for when we say culture, we include the visions, dreams and aspirations of humanity."

Schooling reinforces social distinctions and hierarchies through its 'naturalisation' of a dominant conception of culture in two ways.

1 Through the **negation** of cultural practices that belong to dominated groups and by making the social and cultural history that has given dominance to certain cultural practices 'invisible'.

> The denial of lower, coarse, vulgar, venal, servile - in a word, natural enjoyment - which constitutes the sacred sphere of culture, implies an affirmation of the superiority of those who can be satisfied with the sublimated, refined, disinterested pleasures forever closed to the profane. That is why art and cultural consumption are pre-disposed consciously and deliberately or not, to fulfill a social function of legitimising social differences.
>
> (Bourdieu, 1984)

2 Through **omission**, the liberal progressive tradition in education has tended to treat cultural capital as a 'natural' rather than as a social gift; this is particularly true in terms of literacy. By treating language as a natural gift we have denied many children access to the forms of linguistic capital that some children, because of their social circumstance, are given as a birthright - as the result of a specific upbringing and a specific level of education associated with the elite educational establishments.

Buddy, in Nigel Hinton's novel of the same name, reflects on the injustices of 'upbringing':

> *"As if he didn't look different enough already. Blazer, miles too short at the sleeves. Jeans, instead of grey trousers. ... And a stinking white plastic bag to carry his books and thing ... Sometimes he almost wished he'd never been promoted to the E-stream. E for Express. The top stream. He had been so thrilled at the end of the first year when his class teacher had told him he was going up because his tests had been excellent. E for excellent. It had seemed like the best thing that had ever happened to him. It would have been except - E for Except - he wasn't like the others.*
> *It wasn't just that they all seemed to be able to buy whatever they wanted. It was the way they talked. The things they talked about. The way they casually used names - names of newspapers and books, names of places they'd been to, names of things their parents had bought. They weren't cleverer than he was - in fact some of them were not as clever - but they were different."*

Different. Not inferior/superior, not cleverer/thicker, not better/worse - but different. The difference for Buddy is the difference between those who seem comfortable in the world, knowledgeable about its variety, versed in its customs and rituals, fluent speakers whatever the situation. The difference is not between the *quality* of Buddy's own heritage and experience and that of the other E stream kids - the difference is the breadth and diversity of the other kids' own experience.

As Bourdieu suggests we need:

> *" ... a rational and really universal pedagogy, which would take nothing for granted initially, and would not count as acquired what some and only some of the pupils had inherited, would do all things for all and would be organised with the explicit aim of providing all with the means of acquiring that which, although apparently a natural gift, is only given to the children of the educated classes ... "*

I have lived in Leicester, a Midlands town, for over twenty years. I was a student here. I married and brought up my children in this town. Like many other professional people, I have moved up the property ladder and now live in a small, but expensive, terraced house in a 'desirable' residential area only a few miles from the student flat which was my first home.

At the end of my street there is a private girls' school. Each morning and afternoon there is chaos as cars descend on the street to drop off students. Recently, the school applied for planning permission to expand its numbers. The local councillor sent out letters warning us of the school's plans and giving us details of the proposal. There was outrage in our street. Within days a campaign was mounted, the solicitor across the road prepared a draft letter of objection for us to use and the doctor from number 14 organised a fund to pay for a traffic survey to prove that the daily invasion of cars was a danger to residents and students alike.

When the planning committee met to consider the school's proposals they were faced with seventy five letters of objection - each one detailing the council's legal obligations to provide for the safety of residents and each one making reference to relevant statutes and legal precedence. There was also a persuasive twenty page traffic survey prepared by the same professionals who advise the council. The application was rejected. The school will not expand - because of the objections raised by the people who would have been most affected by the proposed change.

For the last twenty years I have been a regular at the *Manchester Arms*, a pub which is situated near to where I now live. Near but different. The pub is set deep in the back streets of Leicester in a predominantly white working class neighbourhood. The *Manchester Arms* is a large Victorian pub with the best pool room in town. The pool room is upstairs. Downstairs the pub is divided into two quite different spaces. The young people of the neighbourhood use one of these areas - it is loud, busy, smoky. Some of these young people were in the same nursery/kindergarten class as my own son. In the other space there is quiet and decorum; no swearing or horseplay, just the older residents enjoying dominoes and beer. They are separated from their children and grand children by a fifteen foot wall which blocks out the sights and sounds in the next bar. That is the way it has always been in the *Manchester* - at some point in your life you make the journey from one bar to the next and you are replaced by the next generation.

Norman is the landlord. He is an ex-wrestler. Several weeks ago he called out to me and told me that the brewery had decided to close the pub and convert it into a *Mr Q Disco Theme Bar*. The pool room would go, the wall dividing the two bars would go and twenty-four inch TV monitors would beam MTV into the new open-plan bar. Like everyone else in the pub I was shocked by the injustice of a London based brewery deciding to replace the unique culture of the *Manchester* with its own homogenised plastic culture - *Mr Q* bars can be found in every town, the same furniture, the same fizzy beer, the same TV monitors.

We talked about it all night. We made new friends with other regulars who wanted to share their anger. We became nostalgic and told stories of the past - greatnights, eccentric regulars, crazy practical jokes.

I asked Norman when the changes would happen, he told me that there was to be a final meeting on the Thursday and he would let me know when, on the Friday, my regular night for pool. On Friday Norman was excited. He knew the date the pub would close but there had been some excitement at the meeting on Thursday. It had been a planning meeting, Norman explained, and the planning committee delayed its decision for half an hour whilst it considered a letter of objection written by one of the local residents. "Yes" Norman added, "They said if they had had more letters of complaint they would have turned down the brewery's application - pity that isn't' it, if we had known we could have got people writing letters and then we could have kept the pub."

How is it that the people who live in my street know that if you write legal letters and commission traffic surveys you can determine your destiny and that the people who live around the *Manchester* don't? How is that those of us who are already powerful in terms of income, professional status and civic respect already know how to use language to influence events and that those of us who are powerless and poor do not?

The fellow feeling in our street extends beyond literacy resources: as T.S. Eliot remarked, it is a shared 'culture' that provides me with my class identity. Taste is a form of cultural capital - you either have it or you don't.

The sharing of a common culture, whether this involves verbal patterns or artistic experience and objects of admiration, is probably one of the surest foundations of the deep underlying fellow-feeling that unites the members of the governing classes, despite differences of occupation and economic circumstances. It is understandable that TS Eliot should regard culture as the key instrument in the integration of the elite.

(Bourdieu, 1974)

Let us now return to the field of drama/theatre in schools. I want to argue that whenever we talk of the **difference** between drama and theatre we are again both naturalising and neutralising a particular cultural conception of theatre that is literary and class-restricted in its appeal rather than challenging this conception and forging solidarity with artists who are working with alternative conceptions of theatre. The dominant conception of theatre and its selective tradition buries the truth that invention and progress in Western theatre have been closely related to periods of social unrest and change - Athenian, Elizabethan, Victorian, thirties and sixties. New conventions in theatre are not purely aesthetic developments but cultural inventions - periods of social change require new ways of seeing ourselves and the world in which we live.

We reinforce the cultural power of a particular cultural group every time we allow terms like 'proper drama', 'generally accepted ideas about theatre', or even 'from drama to theatre' to go unchallenged in the critiques of the drama in education tradition. 'Proper', 'generally accepted', 'from drama to theatre' or the singular and undifferentiated use of the terms 'culture' and 'aesthetics' are all ways of seducing us into forgetting the complex histories of power in western society. By divorcing drama from the field of theatre we are prevented from challenging the particular conception of theatre that is used as the 'alternative paradigm' in critiques of drama.

The traditional purpose of theatre has been to make visible, and available for critical social debate, the otherwise intangible influences of culture through the physical and local representation of culture **as it is experienced**. Martha Nussbaum (1990), for instance, reminds us of the original purposes of the Greek Tragedy:

To attend a tragic drama was to engage in a communal process of inquiry, reflection and feeling with respect to important civic and personal ends. The very structure of theatrical performance strongly implied this. When we go to the theatre, we usually sit in a darkened auditorium, in the illusion of splendid isolation, while the dramatic action - separated from the spectator by the box of the proscenium arch - is bathed in artificial light as if it were a separate world of fantasy and mystery. The ancient Greek spectator, by contrast, sitting in the common daylight, saw across the staged action the faces of fellow citizens ... And the whole event took place during a solemn civic/religious festival, whose trappings made spectators conscious that the values of the community were being examined and communicated. To respond to these events was to acknowledge and participate in a way of life.

The real difference between the participatory theatres of social action, of which Drama in Education, Theatre in Education and Boal are some examples, and the restricted field of professional theatre is one of contract. In the professional model of theatre there is an economic agreement between players and audiences. The work makes universal claims. The plays of Chekhov and Shakespeare are said to speak to the whole world. The participatory theatres of social action are based on a social contract, a social agreement between a group who gather as potential producers rather than receivers. The meanings that are produced are local to the group and context of production - they make no claims beyond the moment. In this way our work is locally made, local in its relevance and local in its significance and effect. It is made by the people, it is of the people, and it is for the people.

The participatory theatres of social action allow young people to critically examine their local 'habitus'; their own experience of the processes of their own socialisation. It becomes the arena for distinguishing between that which is 'natural' and therefore unchangeable and that which is 'cultural' and therefore transformable. Because it is a theatre of action, a theatre that can only proceed through the actions of the participants, it also provides the forum for rehearsing change at both a personal and social level. Through the processes of theatre, students can explore the seams between nature and culture. They can hold 'morality' up for inspection and represent their own struggles towards private as well as public identities through the problems of representing the 'identities' of others. Through making their own theatre and working with the 'voices' of playwrights, students can make the invisible influence of habitus visible and discussible in all its temporal and spatial specificity.

Above all, we should offer our students a conception of theatre as 'acts of community'; acts of locally produced and received communal representations and, through the processes of production, acts of community making. Theatre in schools should keep alive the possibility of the public theatre of social life by encouraging a local resurrection of the idea of public man and woman.

References

Bourdieu, P. (1974). The School as a Conservative Force. In Eggleton, J. (ed.), *Contemporary Research in the Sociology of Education*. Methuen: London.

Bourdieu, P. & Passeron, J. (1977*)*. *Reproduction in Education, Society and Culture*. Sage: London.

Bourdieu, P. (1984). *Distinction; A Social Critique of the Judgement of Taste*. Harvard University Press: Cambridge, Mass.

Bourdieu, P. (1997). *The Rules of Art*. Polity Press: Cambridge.

Santos-Cabanon, B. (1995). The Power of the Word: Culture, Censorship and Voice. Women's World. PETA.

Bibliography

Bourdieu, P. (1993). *The Field of Cultural Production: Essays on Art and Literature*. Polity Press: Cambridge.

Fraser, N. (1986). Towards a Discourse Ethic of Solidarity. *Praxis International*, 5:4, January.

Geertz, C. (1983). Art as a Cultural System. In *Local Knowledge*. Fontana.

Halliday, M. (1978). *Language as a Social Semiotic*. Arnold: London.

Mouffe, C. (ed) (1992). *Dimensions of Radical Democracy: Pluralism, Citizenship, Community*. Verso: London.

Nussbaum, M. (1990). *Love's Knowledge*. OUP: Oxford.

Passerin d'Entreves, M. (1992). Hannah Arendt and the Idea of Citizenship. In Mouffe, C. (ed), *Dimensions of Radical Democracy: Pluralism, Citizenship, Community*. Verso: London.

Williams, R. (1987). *When was Modernism?* Lecture delivered at University of Bristol, 17/3/87.

Art as a Mode of Knowing

Louise Townend

Geoff Gillham requested that Ms. Towend's article published in the SCYPT Journal, No. 32, Summer 1996, be used as a summary of the nature of the devising workshop he conducted during the weekend. This article is based on a programme directed by Geoff Gillham at the former Belgrade Theatre in Education Company, Coventry.

Proceeding from the philosophical standpoint that the world is knowable, I will be attempting to show how, through the art-form, we can come to know seemingly different aspects of reality in their essence, and in their essential relationship to each other and to the whole. I would like to place three theoretical statements which underpin this article:

(1) The world, which is contradictory and in the process of constant change and movement, is, in all its aspects, governed by the laws of nature - the process of which is dialectical. Engels (1996) writes of the necessity of dialectical thinking in attempting to know the world, thinking which grasps things, images, ideas, essentially in their interconnection, in their sequence, in their movement, their birth and death.

(2) In his book, *The Psychology of Art,* Vygotsky (1978) is concerned with the relationship between art and life, and in moving towards an evaluation of art he is in accordance with the view that art is an original, chiefly emotional dialectical approach to building life. He approaches the subject from the psychological viewpoint that a work of art itself is an indispensable discharge of nervous energy and a complex method of finding an equilibrium between our organism and the environment in critical instances of our behaviour.

(Vygotsky, 1978)

(3) For those perceiving art, he writes that it introduces the effects of passion, violates inner equilibrium and changes will in a new sense ...

(Vygotsky, 1978)

In the light of Vygotsky's theory I hope to begin to explore how art, as operating in the area of feeling, can move both the artist and the beholder towards knowing, and its significance in the overall process of growth in human beings. I shall refer, for examples, to the devising work I observed in the early summer of 1988 in the Coventry Belgrade Theatre in Education youth and community project, *When Sleeping Dogs Awake.* They were devising work which would be done for ten to twelve year olds and for their parents in evening performances of the play.

From the outset the team's aim was to present a show about racism and, for the purposes of exploring the subject, they drew a distinction between: *racist ideas and actions in the day-to-day lives of ordinary people,* which they referred to as 'street racism'; and the *objective position of racism and racist ideology in the actual mechanics of capitalism, colonialism and imperialism,* which they referred to as 'systemic racism'. In having drawn the clear distinction between them, they set themselves the goal to explore and trace the connection between the one and the other. They did so with a view to helping the children do the same thing via the play they devised and the drama workshops which would follow it. These aims were developed, in the course of two or three discussions, from their initial impulse to deal with racism in the context of the economic and social history of Coventry. As I shall show, the aims of the programme underwent a further transformation at a later stage in the devising process as a result of discussions arising from the practical/artistic exploration.

Devising is learning

Having established, by discussion, a line of enquiry for themselves - to trace the connections between 'street' and 'systemic' racism - the company immediately began to work in the art-form. The historical and documentary research that another company might have engaged in at this stage was specifically ruled out by the director in setting up the first exercise. With the barest historical detail, the team were asked to depict a scene involving the execution of an Indian rebel during the Indian Mutiny. The first depiction was the tying of the Indian to the end of a canon by an Indian soldier under the command of an English Commanding Officer, just prior to its being fired. The second was the moment immediately after the firing of the canon. The third was after the Commanding Officer had left the scene and the Indian soldier cleaned the canon. (Each was given separately). Each depiction was accompanied by a simple narration of the moment or by a vocalising of the thoughts of each of the men. In this exercise was contained, in embryonic form, the whole development of the programme (as it later turned out), and the essence of coming to know through the art-form. The director's brief was for the team to try and show *how it was,* i.e. to utilise their intuitive sense of what it is to be human and moreover, without moral judgements or their ideas about the situation interposing themselves. Through the use of their feelings about an emotionally horrifying and sharply contradictory event, but in a very cool mode, they were able, in Dorothy Heathcote's phrase, to get 'close to the absolute guts of the event.'

The product of this exercise was questions like: 'What was stopping the soldier from recognising his own and the mutineer's interests as being common?' 'What has to happen to someone to enable them to carry out atrocities?' It revealed very clearly the discrepancy between the subjective thoughts of the soldier and the objective position he was in. Already the contradictions contained in the work were beginning to yield questions to drive further exploration, particularly with regard to the relationship between 'street' and 'systemic' racism.

It is extremely unlikely that the depth of questioning of the world would have been achieved or so quickly, through discussion or historical research - both of which operate principally in the cognitive rather than the affective mode.

From the first exercise an important equation can be drawn out. The process of devising (in the art-form) is a process of learning. Conventionally, the process of devising has been seen as the process of finding a form to teach what you already know.

At a later point, when the team were looking for the unanswered questions that would provide the cutting edge of the play, they were asked to list what were, for them, the 'warm trails' (i.e. points of concern or disturbance), and to place them as concrete images or actions, not as ideas. For example:

1. Kitchen labourer (black) speaks to youth (also black), knowing and not knowing how it is to be black in Britain.
2. The man who was once a farmer who grew the hemp for the rope which now binds him to the canon.
3. Villagers in India see their first train.
4. A woman writes a sign for her boarding-house: *No blacks, no Jews, no dogs.*
5. A man draws a plan for the stowage of slaves - 18th century.
6. An Indian farmer, pleased to do business with an employee of the East India Company.

Out of the suggested images, twelve were selected to which the response was 'warmest'. The task then was to draw out the contradictions contained in the images, those that were common to all of them and, in doing so, to find the essential: the essence. Having found in discussion what they considered to be the unanswered question they were then asked to create a scene which would pose that question. Taking as their starting point their own emotional response to material thrown up in the course of the work, the team (in groups) went about finding the form that would point to the universals. One depiction showed the moment (reported in the film, *Shoah*) when a Jewish barber was faced with having to cut the hair of his wife as she passed him on the way to the gas chamber. The team were asked to place, as they watched each other's work, what they felt to be the questions arising out of the pieces. Of this particular depiction the question arose:

Under what conditions do people say enough is enough?

The interaction of form with content, and vice versa

This method of working with and through the art-form - consciously working with concrete images and particulars and allowing the meaning of the thing to show itself through the form, is entirely in keeping with the natural process of coming to know a given phenomenon. We are, in everyday life, constantly confronted with many forms and in watching these in their movement, are able, if we don't get side-tracked into our ideas of what they are, to come to know their essential content. In the case of the devising process, the working through of images (the forms) was integral to the development of the team's understanding of the concrete content of the connection of 'street racism' and 'systemic racism'. Equally, each new content question drove the team into a deeper exploration of the form of the content.

From the depiction work around the canon had arisen the question of how the rope which tied the man to the canon got there: 'what was its life history?' In the course of that work, rope was explored as a particular, mobile image expressing the history of colonialism in India, from its origin as a product produced by a farmer from his own hemp for his own use, through to rope as commodity manufactured from a cash crop and sold under the monopoly control of the (British) East India Company. This began to enrich the content of the question posed earlier, 'What was stopping the soldier from recognising his own and the mutineer's interests as being common?' (see 'warm trail' 2, above). The rope was moving from being an 'accidental' prop in the action of a scene, to a rich and 'necessary' holding-form for the chain of connections implicit in the concepts of the programme. The recognition of this 'necessity' led the team to consider rope as a potential central image for a historical play developing around the rope industry; to tie in colonialism in India with capitalism now and immigrant labour in the post-war period in Coventry.

With that content possibility in mind, the company began work on the metaphoric possibilities in rope. There was a sense amongst the team that the qualities of rope, its uses in society, and the resonance it carried around the notion of 'oppression' would have a generative value for the exploration of the content. The team were given the following titles in turn and asked to spend ten minutes working towards a one-minute showing of each. They were asked to use a moving depiction in relation to which the title itself would play an active part:

'Roped in';

'The knot strains against itself';

'The intertwining of many strands makes the thin rope very strong';

'Shall they cut the rope or untie the knot?':

'The rope is fraying and they do not see'.

The depictions around the first title, 'Roped in', touched particularly on the question: 'how do people come to act as they do?' There was exploration of peer group pressure, of being conned into doing something and ending up being exploited, and how the rewards and benefits of certain actions often outweigh the risk of considering alternatives. All of the depictions were worked on bearing in mind the exploration of the interrelationship of 'street racism' to 'systemic racism,' and they fed into the discussion on how people come to be divided against each other, and whose interests are ultimately served. Because of the nature of the titles, the depictions looked closely at oppression and its equal and opposite reaction in the drive towards ending it.

Through the practice, the team's own thinking was developing around the notion of cause and effect, and the unity of the two as regards oppression, particularly in relation to the concept of class relation. The contradictions were contained around the image of rope itself and the work generated was very rich, stimulated by the team's artistic sense of its 'rightness'.

It was in this particular work that the team chanced on what was to become the central metaphor for the programme. One of the scenes shown in relation to the title, 'The rope is fraying and they do not see,' showed a dog on a long lead, led by his master, a sturdy representation of British Imperialism. Whilst he chatted with another, the dog chewed furiously at the rope, stopping only when his master turned. The image of the dog was both effective and delightful, and, at a later point, the team began to discuss the potential metaphoric value of 'dogs'. But this was only after exploring many other images and particulars such as detailed dramatic reconstructions of black team members' direct experience of 'street racism'. In addition, the team had to consider (and kept considering!) how their aims could be met with regard to racism if they took so oblique an angle on it by focusing on 'dogs'. In the event, this became less important to the team as their aims underwent their final transformation:

1. How do material conditions affect people's thoughts and actions?
2. How is it that people frequently hold ideas contrary to their real interests?

These questions underlay the initial research for the connections between 'street racism' and 'systemic racism', waiting to be discovered and abstracted. In developing the dog metaphor, the point of departure in the aims to teach about racism was never far away as the particular, manifesting a deeper essence: the relationship between consciousness and social being contained in the two questions.

The metaphor of dogs is rich enough to generate those questions of itself. It contains within it, for example, the relationship of dogs to their owners; the significance of the lead; the nature of their training in different situations; the way they are separated from each other; their social instinct; their trust in their owners; their capacity to be savage; etc. For example, gathering around the notion of the 'dogness' of people and the 'human-ness' of dogs, their domestication and training, their group instinct and common interest, the team decided to follow their 'noses' and explore practically its generative value. A group improvisation was set up, centred on a racist attack (which had been explored earlier in human terms) in which one member of the team played the owner, representing the capitalist class, and another played the dog-trainer representing the educators and the media, whilst the others played dogs. Later, the question of how the various dogs came to be as they were was addressed through working on scenes showing the relationship between the dog and their trainer, and how they were trained. Echoes of the work on rope emerged as these titles were followed:

'When the lead is first put on'
'When the lead is taken off'

Watching the actors at work I found the scenes sometimes funny, in the recognition of the truth in them; sometimes sad; and, at other times, ominous. Everyone was in agreement that for the age-range (10-12 year olds), dogs would have an appeal and that, in working towards a concrete scenario, the possibilities would be there for holding all the relevant areas of learning in an economic form. The metaphor had not arisen out of an idea as such, but out of the organic process in which the use of concepts for analysis and exploration of sensuous concrete reality featured in unity. At every point the team drew on aspects of the objective world from the past and the present, making connections and working with their own affective responses to the material to draw together a sensuous representation of the world and all its contradictions.

Before moving on to discuss the role of art in knowing for the audience, I shall draw out a few principles of devising that particularly struck me as an observer of Belgrade's method of artistic exploration with *When Sleeping Dogs Awake*: the necessity of:

a) recognising the contradictory nature of the world;
b) recognising oneself as part of that;
c) confronting those difficulties presented in a real way, that is to say, without obliterating the contradictions;
d) working concretely to explore 'how things are' and not how we *think* they are;
e) finding the unanswered questions in order to deepen understanding;
f) allowing one's sensuous response to the world to guide one's artistic practice;
g) working to understand theoretically the laws by which the world, and art within it, moves;
h) working consciously to develop those theoretical understandings *in relation* to the practice itself.

How art works on the beholder

On entering the world of dogs through the theatre form, the audience will also be faced with a world of human beings. In *Towards A Theory of Instruction*, Bruner (1966) writes that the "power of a representation can be described as its capacity in the hands of a learner, to connect matters that on the surface seem quite separate" and, on art, he writes that:

"the principle of economy of art produces the compact image or symbol that by its genius travels great distances to connect ostensible disparities".

(Bruner, 1966)

Finding a metaphor is not a simple case of finding a neat parallel: if that were so we would be in the area of ideas, replacing one particular with another.

When Bruner (1966) speaks of the 'compact image', he is referring to its resonance on every level and points to its capacity to systematise knowledge for the onlooker. In being able to begin categorising particulars by the use of organising concepts, the learner can start to develop an understanding of the details of which the total picture is composed; and, at the same time, get a clearer picture of the nature of the whole. The power of art to do so is bound up in its economy as, through the use of metaphor, theconfounding inessentials in life fall away, revealing the complexities of nature in a reasonably simple form.

83

In watching a piece of theatre, the audience is free to take a relationship to what is presented. When referring to art generally, Vygotsky (1978) points out that the working through of an affective response is a creative act on the part of the onlooker, in an effort to overcome and resolve the feelings generated. Put another way, this could be seen as an expression of the will to learn; and, if the questions are worth asking, then the desire to know and to engage with the content will be stimulated.

In Bruner's theory of instruction his first point is that it is through the arousal of curiosity that the desire to know is activated. Following on from that, he considers that there must be something to maintain the interest. His third point is that the potential benefits must exceed the risks involved in subsequent exploration of the material. Lastly, there must be something to keep the work from being random, i.e. a task which will direct the learner's exploration of his/her response to the material in relation to a known goal.

When writing on the response of the beholder, Bruner (1966) writes:

"Two types of cognitive activity are set in train when a need is aroused. One is at the centre of awareness as desire. It is directed toward achieving an end and is specialised to the task of finding means. The other is at the fringe of awareness, a flow of rich and surprising fantasy, a tangled reticle of associations that give fleeting glimpses of past occasions, of disappointments and triumphs, of pleasures and unpleasures".

The programme

The play itself begins with the killing of one stray dog by another. In the course of the play, the audience is shown the nature of dogs, their actions, the conditions in which they are living, and the relationship of the one to the other. The final scene shows them still arguing with one another, not fully understanding their position, right up to the last moment when the dog wardens arrive to catch them for extermination. The contradiction in the first scene is still present in the last, centring around the question: 'what did the dogs need to know in order to act in their own best interests?' The audience is left with the need to resolve the unresolved.

Bruner's (1966) third point about the benefits of the learning exceeding the risks involved related to an important feature of the art-form, that of its being 'other' to the pupils.

The metaphor of the dogs came out of the devising process which necessarily contained an analysis of the world we live in. It also looked to the particulars in the world and, in exploring the relationship of the two, found a metaphor which would embody both and their interconnectedness. It is because the process was as such that what the theatre produced was bound to be a truthful representation of the world. The pupils themselves, also part of that world, will recognise the world in the resonant metaphor and yet, at the same time, have an enabling distance to the content. The power of art to prompt the learner to grapple with experience and knowledge, and to begin to order it for themselves, is enhanced by the unity of the safety of its distance and the draw of its proximity.

The follow-up work of the pupils involved producing a memorial exhibition through which to warn other dogs of the danger of their position. They are to become involved in the action of the play, drawn into the world of dogs, at the same time as processing for themselves the new knowledge contained in the play. In working with the metaphor they will be trying out possible action to take in the real world. Vygotsky (1978) writes of the power of such engagement:

"By dragging a child into a topsy-turvy world we help his intellectual work, because the child becomes interested in creating such a topsy-turvy world for himself in order to become more effectively master of the laws governing the real world. These absurdities could be dangerous for a child if they screened out the real interrelationships between ideas and objects. Instead they push them to the fore and emphasise them. They enhance (rather than weaken) the child's perception of reality."

Vygotsky (1978) likens the instruction-development relationship to that of the play-development relationship at pre-school age, characterised by a subordination to rules which, for the child creates the demand to act against immediate impulse. "Play", he writes,

"is the source of development, and creates the zone of proximal development. Action in the imaginative sphere, in an imaginary situation, the creation of voluntary intention and the formation of real-life plans and volitional motives - all appear in play and make it the highest level of pre-school development."

The testing out of new meaning, in such a way that the child is placed in an empowered position to act in relation to it, is a natural process. In play, the zone of proximal development is created unconsciously by the child: in instruction, it must be created consciously by the teacher, whose structuring of knowledge enables the child to be guided towards understanding that which is just out of reach, but not too far out of their grasp as to be impossible to attain. There is an obvious similarity here between the action in play, and the action that the pupils involved in the theatre programme will be engaged in. With the help of their teachers and the actor/teachers, the pupils will be addressing the universal questions through the concrete actions they take and the decisions they make concerning the production of the exhibition. Working in the drama mode, the pupils will be working through their own affective responses to the material operating with the learning areas embedded in the play. Later in their school work, the pupils will be guided towards an application of their own learning in relation to the particular of racism. Bruner's (1966) thinking on the resulting effectiveness of any learning structure is that it is to be seen in the learner's capacity to apply it to the world.

"I suspect that much of growth starts out by turning around on our own traces and recoding in new form with the aid of adult tutors what we have been doing or seeing, then going on to the new modes of organisation with the new products that have been formed by these recodings. We say 'I see what I am doing now'."

Bruner's theory of instruction is based on Vygotsky's investigative work into the natural process of learning. For Vygotsky, the action of art itself is a movement towards knowing, and its purpose is to enable human beings to master the natural laws to which they are also subject. It is a movement towards growth, itself in accordance with those laws and, as such, a natural tool to be used in the process of moving from a lower to a higher order of control of existence. What separates human beings from animals is the making and use of tools: the development of concepts as tools with which to order experience is an essential feature in the process of knowing. The individual is naturally predisposed to learning: naturally curious. The desire to know can be activated, and the process of coming to know sharpened and guided through the arts in education. Vygotsky (1978) writes:

Art is the organisation of our future behaviour. It is a requirement that may never be fulfilled but that forces us to strive beyond our life toward all that lies beyond it.

References

Bruner, J.S. (1966). *Toward a Theory of Instruction.* Cambridge, Mass.: Belknap Press of Harvard University Press.

Lea, J. (ed.) (1996). *The Condition of Britain: Essays on Frederick Engels.* London: Pluto.

Vygotsky, L.S. (1978). Mind in Society: the Development of Higher Psychological Processes. Cambridge, Mass.: Harvard University Press.

Research and the Teaching of Drama

John Somers

John Somers is a Senior Lecturer in the School of Education, University of Exeter. He is Founding Editor of the international journal Research in Drama Education and director of the biennial conference Researching Drama and Theatre in Education.

In the field of drama and theatre in Education, wisdom that has been so painstakingly gathered by the pioneers and those that have succeeded them, has often been lost or scattered, trapped within national boundaries, stored at the commercial whim of publishers, or broadcast in ways that make it difficult for people to consider it. The result is that, unlike those in other disciplines, we often do not design or conduct our research in ways that build on our community's acquired knowledge. We are not fully aware of the day-to-day incremental advances in knowledge or the inspirational leaps of understanding, with the result that much of the hard-won enlightenment is as ephemeral as the drama process that generated it.

I wrote that in the first editorial in the journal *Research in Drama Education* published in 1996. I started the journal as I felt that were few depositories where we could store and make available our acquired wisdom. The enthusiastic response to the first four issues of the journal seems to prove that this was a widespread belief.

I also wrote that we lacked a settled research tradition and that we had far too long been in thrall to the gurus that had traditionally dominated our advances. It was time, I thought, for us to get out from under the potentially immobilising influence of the few and to recognise the need for a wider series of research activities, rooted mainly in the practice of drama, encouraging a broad, confident band of teachers and practitioners to make and share their own enquiry.

I still believe that. The ground cannot be covered solely by academics and the relatively small percentage of teachers who are doing research degrees. Research must become a common tradition, one that can support, revitalise and develop the practice of drama.

I came in for some criticism for those comments. Some argued that teachers were already engaged in research and that reflective practice was such a widespread phenomenon that I misrepresented the situation. I recognise the work done by individual teachers as valuable in advancing their practice, but we need a wider range of research activity than this reflection generates. One of the criteria that I would apply to research, for example, is that, if possible, its outcomes need to be made available to others. This might involve sharing them with other staff in the school or presenting the outcomes at an international conference or in a professional or research journal. It does not much matter where as long as the forum is apposite, but we do need to share and debate the findings if we are to build a secure base and superstructure for our art.

Why research?

Knowledge is power and research brings knowledge and with it, understanding. There is a growing corpus of pure drama practice in the world and we have long escaped the narrow, restrictive and prescriptive notions of what drama is and how it should be taught - eclecticism is in the air. And after thirty-four years of teaching drama in a variety of situations I am also excited by the internationalisation of drama communication. We are finding strength and confidence in knowing that drama is, in most places, growing and where not growing, at least holding its own. And yet I am convinced that we need to engage more systematically in research if we are to understand even more about drama and build an irrefutable argument for its inclusion in the curricula of the world's education systems. As part of that process, research must take place in every corner in which drama functions. With the results of a review of the National Curriculum due in the year 2000, we have little time to waste.

Who should be doing it?

We all know that most who work in Higher Education have a contractual requirement to do research. It forms one third of our job (with teaching and administration the other two thirds), and is increasingly important as the ratings received by departments for research have a profound effect on the moneys made available to that department. The nature and organisation of research differs widely. At the base level, individuals conduct research with little or no funding. This is especially so in the Arts, where enquiry can be conducted on a low cost basis with little more than a tape recorder and camera. At the other end of the scale, and particularly in the sciences, large teams of researchers are supported by multi-million pound grants and complex equipment.

As stated earlier, most teachers are involved in kinds of research. It is a necessary part of their function as they unscramble the daily experience of teaching and build the knowledge accrued into their future practice. This is the world of the reflective practitioner, although at first glance most teachers would not characterise it as research. What most would more readily recognise as research are the kinds of work that many are doing towards obtaining a masters or PhD qualification. These people choose a particular question or focus and have the benefit of a supervisor with whom they can discuss their work. What we must develop is the territory between these two to achieve a more widespread research ethos in schools - one that may or may not be hitched into a higher degree route (although if teachers are doing work that could lead to a higher degree, why shouldn't they get credit for it?).

In 1972, *The James Report* recognised the invaluable role of research for teachers:

Many witnesses (to the Committee of Enquiry) *have urged the importance of wider opportunities for research for practising teachers ... Teachers who particularly wish to take part in this kind of activity should have in-service opportunities to familiarise themselves with research techniques.*

Many of the James' recommendations were never implemented. Margaret Thatcher received it as Secretary of State, so perhaps that is not so surprising. In fact, a Universities' Council for the Education of Teachers survey shows that after a peak in the mid-1980s of 2,200 teachers being granted secondment to universities for Masters degrees and other forms of studies, that number fell to 650 in 1988, the first year after Local Management of Schools was introduced. The following year it declined to 400 and the year after that to 200, almost all of whom were educational psychology trainees who were funded separately.[1]

So if the growth area is in schools and we are not in the happy position posited by James, how do we bridge that gap between the individual reflective practitioner and the university registered research student? Is it possible for a research culture to grow amongst drama teachers that is largely self-supporting and where the research outcomes are disseminated widely within and outside the profession? This may already be the case in other countries, but if it is to take place in the UK it will require a change of attitude to what constitutes teaching. Currently, teachers in the UK spend almost all of their time with groups of students or preparing to teach them or assessing and recording the work produced. This leaves them little time or, in truth, energy to engage in more than a modicum of research and most of that is utilitarian and needs led. What we require is a view of the teacher's role as multifaceted, involving only, say, two thirds of the week in the company of students and some of the rest of that time being devoted to other professional matters, including research and the dissemination and discussion of its outcomes. The current model of teaching is based on the relatively simple teacher approaches of 19th Century instruction and learning by rote, and it is inappropriate for the sophisticated operations to be found in the school of the 21st Century.

Such change will cost money and it is not likely to happen in the short term, but this is an objective for which teachers in the UK need to strive. We require time to visit other schools, to share notions of theory and practice and to observe and evaluate the work of other teachers. This will not happen unless teachers demand it. For too long we have waited for the policy initiatives to come from on high - increasingly, as a result of eighteen years of conservative rule, with a large political, ideological label attached. It was the Conservatives who abolished the Schools Council and imposed the bureaucracy of curriculum control and it was the teachers who struggled to make the National Curriculum work when, by all the laws of justice, its incongruencies and glaring inadequacies should have led to its withdrawal. If such change is to happen, we will need to take concerted action. The proposed General Teaching Council would be a step in the right direction, but we need to go much further than that. Teachers need to take the initiative, to assert, as do other professions, that only (or mainly) they have the professional knowledge that can allow them to work out the strategies and approaches for effective education. Then we may be able to integrate a research tradition into the daily work of teaching. In the short and medium term we need strategies that move us along that road.

The best way of introducing this research culture might be to integrate it into teacher education. In fact many institutions do this. In my own School of Education, for example, we have a long tradition of requiring students to conduct a form of research in both their second and fourth year school experiences. The first requires them to investigate some aspect of their own practice, to evaluate it and reflect on the process in a written account that is discussed with teachers in the school, supervising tutor and main subject tutor. This topic is practically based and chosen by the student in consultation with school and university. In the fourth year, the investigation is more sophisticated and it usually centres on a question. In my own area of English and Drama, for example, students have investigated such issues as:

- Is publication of students' stories in a bound volume an effective way of giving added value to their work?
- Can daily reading aloud by students of self-chosen poems lead to a greater love and appreciation of poetry?
- Are children's stories an effective starting point for making drama?
- What emphasis should be placed on knowledge of form in Primary Drama?
- How can the preparation of a primary school assembly make best use of drama skills?

The outcomes are often enthralling and of great use to students in developing their emerging practice. I have read some inspirational work and much of it is of publishable quality (one piece is currently in preparation for publication in a professional journal, for example). The requirement that more and more of teacher education move into schools could pose a threat to this tradition of research. Schools, as previously stated, do not generally see research as a requirement and it is unlikely, therefore, that such work will expand or even be protected. Now that at least two thirds of a Post Graduate Certificate in Education course must be situated in schools, it will be more difficult for universities to stimulate and protect the 'enquiry' element of those students' teacher education. The initiative, therefore, must come from schools.

So what might be done in the short and medium term? I know the pressure teachers are under, so I am under no illusion about the difficulty of their implementing any of this, even if they so wished. But how about:

- Encouraging each teacher to investigate some aspect of their practice over the course of a year. Outcomes of that research could then be shared with other teachers in that school in a series of professional development, non-pupil days.
- Schools deciding through a process of consultation, their priorities for research investigations and developing strategies to carry them out.

- Establishing a network of contacts and professional liaisons to allow teachers and schools to share the outcomes with colleagues in other schools
- Publishing a digest of research in progress to allow teachers and others, including those in universities, to be aware of work in progress.

All of this should be properly integrated into a professional development pattern and resourced to allow teachers supported time away from the classroom to further their research. Universities will have to be flexible about the kinds of awards they make and how they can be achieved. Maximum flexibility through modular and other schemes and credit transfer will be required to serve the needs of teachers, and universities will have to provide consultants who can work in schools to advise and to act as sounding boards.

New ways of disseminating outcomes of research must be found with the internet playing an important part. Subject associations could be helpful in co-ordinating and communicating national and international outcomes. In the UK, National Drama and The National Association for the Teaching of Drama could take the lead in making some of this happen on a more regular and secure basis. With members from across all phases of the profession, they are in an ideal position to set up working parties that would get things started. We ought to re-establish the long-cherished notion that teachers should be entitled to sabbatical leave. Way back in 1972 *The James Report* said:

> *The immediate aim should be to secure teachers' entitlement to the minimum of one term or the equivalent for every seven years, but this should be regarded only as an interim target. As soon as possible, the level of entitlement should be raised to one term in five years.*

Above all as a profession we need to seize the initiative. Because of the resource implications and the potential shifting of the locus of power, no one is going to hand it to us on a plate - it will have to be fought for on an incremental basis.

I stress that teachers must decide what is to be investigated. It is not for policy makers, politicians or universities to dictate, although they may have an important function in some aspects of the process. As with research generally, the projects will range across the spectrum - conducted by an individual teacher of drama over the course of one term for sharing with a colleague; a whole department in a secondary school that chooses to investigate a particular issue over a one-year period; research conducted by teams of teachers in two schools for subsequent sharing; a three-year nation-wide investigation on a matter of national priority.

I know that there are already models in operation in particular schools and that there are many instances of exciting co-operation between teachers and universities, but I am pretty sure that these are not widespread practices. We need action to make them so and with a change of government now is the time to get it rolling. Tony Blair has said that his Government's priorities are 'Education, Education Education!', so let's take him at his word. The early omens were not good. Within days of taking office, David Blunkett alleged that teachers had 'lost their way', had been seduced by 'trendy methods'. I doubt whether he had any more evidence than the previous administration on which to base these assumptions, but it is yet one more example of teachers being told what is wrong with their work. It is time that teachers were in a position to counter the assertions of transitory political voices with evidence, evidence culled from respected, rigorous enquiry.

At the moment the bulk of the £70 million that is spent annually on educational research is made available to researchers to conduct enquiry that they see as important. The head of the Office for Standards in Education, Chris Woodhead, has just ordered a study of educational research over the last four years and its impact on classroom practice and whether it is subject to political bias (Murphy, 1996). It may not be long before the bulk of that money is reserved for research commissioned by Ofsted and like bodies. Teachers need to become capable of originating and conducting their *own* research projects, reflecting *their* priorities before the money becomes locked up in quango-land.

What sort of issues should teachers be researching?

The simple answer is anything that intrigues them and about which they wish to gain greater understanding. The list is pretty endless. Here are a few that would catch my interest:

- Why is it that some students seem to come alive in Drama and have a special affinity for it?
- Given the difficulty of the labour market and the general lack of parental understanding of what it is, why does drama remain so popular with students?
- What sort of learning takes place in drama?
- What is the relationship of the dramatic form to the material that is dramatised?
- Does it matter what we do Drama about?
- How should we assess Drama?
- What records should be kept of students' achievements in Drama?
- How can those records be of real use to the students and to those who will teach them Drama in the future?
- What constitutes 'progression' in Drama?
- How is a devised performance made?
- What benefits flow from a school play production?
- Is Drama work enhanced by the availability of specific props, costumes and staging, or are more generic materials of more use?
- What kinds of productive relationships can be made between Drama and Art/Music/Dance?
- What are parents' and other teachers' perceptions of Drama?
- What sort of material seems to work best with each age group?
- How should or can the drama teacher intervene in students' drama work?

- How best can a teacher operate teacher in role?
- What particular skills and operations are in use by a teacher of Drama compared to those of the classroom teacher?
- What happens to the more able Drama students when they leave school?

To investigate any one of these questions, one would need to produce a research design, a grand term for working out how to approach finding some of the answers. To do this effectively means, ideally, having access to a range of research methods and choosing those that might yield material that can be pondered. But lack of such comprehensive knowledge should not stop us getting started. If I want to mend a puncture on my bike, I do not have to know all about the twenty-one gear train or the lever systems of the brakes, although I will if I wish to become a fully trained and skilled cycle mechanic. We begin research like most other things we take up - by learning a bit at a time, acquiring those skills we need to know to carry out a particular operation. So I urge teachers to get started, undaunted by their, possibly incomplete knowledge. Ideally, they should find another person who shares their curiosity and with whom they can discuss what they are doing and what seems to be coming out of it. Using one or two key books that may give them some guidance and contact people outside their school who may assist them in framing their questions or discovering how to dig up some answers.

Outside teaching

In addition to investigation in teaching, we need a culture of enquiry in other areas of dramatic activity. Theatre in Education has seen the number of its constituent companies dwindle alarmingly in the UK over the past fifteen years. To a large degree that was as a result of political antipathy or malign intent by the Conservatives. They saw TIE as at best irrelevant and at worst a dangerous tool for allowing students to think about controversial issues. But we lacked the well founded evidence with which to argue the case. Why is it that TIE can be an effective educational tool? What unique qualities <u>does</u> it have that make it an essential ingredient of a balanced education? How best can the autonomy of professional artists be maintained whilst making TIE a more valuable resource for schools?

The political fights were impressive and TIE and its representative organisations fought hard - but its lockers were too empty of evidence of the kind that would sway those that were making the policy decisions and, most importantly, allocating funding.

Another area we need to research is that of the potential for drama and theatre to contribute to the development of individuals from the cradle to the grave, from infant drama classes, to visiting puppet shows, to school productions, to TIE, to professional theatre outreach programmes, to A level Theatre Studies, to university Drama courses, to Arts centre activity, to repertory theatres and the National Theatre. Such studies would explore the notion that drama forms a seamless web of activity and constitutes an essential ingredient in our culture without which we would not only be impoverished, but probably be heading for psychological ill-health. Our aim should be to obtain from the Government, Arts Council, Local Authorities *et al.*, a commitment to support the huge complex matrix of drama activity that is embedded in our culture. If we are to succeed <u>we</u> must do the spade work - collect and process the evidence, prepare and organise the forums where discussion can take place, place judicious pressure in areas that will bring about change. There is a woeful ignorance of the breadth of wealth that the Arts bring to this country but no one will take up the cudgels unless we do.

Rolling the rock

So, if we believe that this is a valid aim, how <u>do</u> we get going? When I was in Secondary teaching there was an understanding that you needed to operate at a higher level for a period before the school management recognised that you were worthy of promotion. Few gained it because of their potential. In the same way, even given the crowded and often exhausting schedule that constitutes teaching in a modern school, we may need to prove we can do this research and that it enhances the education of our students and us as teachers, before we can gain official recognition and witness policy change. We would need to argue the case through professional organisations and the, hopefully, soon to be established General Teaching Council, by means of our political affiliations and within our schools - with the management and with colleagues. We must be prepared to counter the sceptical views of our colleagues towards research and challenge the argument that there are no resources to support such work. We may have to start small, but we need to establish the principles.

To begin with, research may not be properly resourced and this will require some colleagues being supportive and tolerant of others' efforts to conduct investigation on the understanding that the compliment will be returned. But let's get going. And remember, research is not some esoteric activity engaged in as a sideline to practice. It is central to our development of practice and through it we become better teachers and practitioners.

I would be happy to see responses to this polemic. What do you think is the place of research? Do you see it as a necessary part of a teacher's function. If you are a teacher in schools, do you do it and, if so, what are you researching? Are the ideas expressed here conceived in cloud cuckoo land or do you see in them the seeds of proper professional advance? What is to be done?

References

HMSO (1972). *Teacher Education and Training*. The James Report. HMSO: London, pp. 9-10.

Murphy, R. (1996). The Evidence in the Classroom. *Guardian Education*, 16 October 1996, p. 6.

Notes

1.   Figures obtained from Professor Ted Wragg, who conducted the survey for UCET.

Readers interested in the international journal *Research in Drama Education* and/or the biennial conference *Researching Drama and Theatre in Education*, can contact John Somers at The University of Exeter, School of Education, Exeter, Devon, EX1 2LU; Tel: 01392 264824; email <J.W.Somers@ex.ac.uk>

Opening the Gap and Inserting the Contradiction

Bogusia Matusiak-Varley

Bogusia Matusiak-Varley is an Educational Consultant and a Registered Inspector.

The purpose of this article is to share with drama teachers and heads of department a user friendly interpretation of the Ofsted framework in order to highlight the contribution that drama makes to the whole of the inspection process. In so doing I hope to help teachers facilitate the process of inspection both for themselves and for inspectors, so that both can gain a deeper insight into the nature of drama and the contribution it can make to developing a humanised curriculum.

I find myself in a very privileged position having had extensive experience both as a drama practitioner at primary and university level and as a schools' registered inspector. This has enabled me to recognise that there are areas of communication that need to be improved in order to open up a more effective dialogue about the nature of drama, the quality of teaching and learning, the contribution that drama makes to the school ethos and the impact that drama skills can have on raising the levels of pupils' attainment across the curriculum. It is becoming clear from informal conversations that I have had with inspectors that it is very difficult to inspect drama when there are so many variances in school as to what the nature of drama is and how it is taught and organised. Often the document presented to the team of inspectors is vague in content as to exactly how the school views drama and the methods that are used to both gather assessments and assess progress.

At present, drama teachers can make the most significant impact to the inspection process by providing detailed information about drama within their school, in the documentation that is sent to inspectors prior to the inspection. In this article I will be dissecting the Ofsted framework requirements and I will be inserting questions for consideration for the drama teacher. By presenting the requirements of Ofsted I would like to think that I could allay the fear of inspection so that drama practitioners can carry on with the process of quality teaching in their lessons and not be strait-jacketed into thinking that their work might not meet Ofsted requirements. No humanised curriculum can evolve in a climate of fear. Fear paralyses creativity and in my role as registered inspector I have seen numerous teachers play safe during the week of inspection and teach mediocre lessons because they are afraid to take risks just in case this is not what the inspector wants to see. I hope that the ensuing information will allay those fears and that teachers will continue to do what they know best: that is to teach according to the pupils' needs in a challenging and interesting way.

The summer of 1997 has been action packed for registered inspectors with

with courses relating to improving the process of inspection. The inspection process will be closely monitored by HMI who will report on the way the inspection has been run. Negative feed back will result in many of us losing our jobs, therefore inspectors' stress levels will be high in an attempt at meeting very stringent quality control criteria. Inspectors are advised to spend less time in lessons and more time scrutinising pupils' work. The usual criteria of providing more information in less time will create problems as less time will be spent in classrooms and judgements on standards will be gleaned from pupils' written work or photographic evidence! **Alarm bells**!!! The best drama lessons involve action, and writing is not necessarily always produced. The essence of dramatic tension cannot always be captured in a photograph!

With this type of system in operation, my responsibility for managing the inspection in school has highlighted the need to further develop the type of partnerships with schools which ensure that the inspection can be seen as a useful and valid process for all concerned and that all the evidence that teachers want to present to us can be seen in the very short time scale which is allocated to us.
(I apologise for the use of **WE** but in this article I cannot disassociate myself from the two professional hats that I wear.)

How do we as drama teachers survive in a system which, in many cases, is contrary to our beliefs and does not understand the intricacies of our work?

How do we convince the unenlightened as to the value of what we do? How do we place the child at the centre of our work within a legal framework which does not fully understand the subtleties of our practice? It is with these questions in mind that I started to think about how best I could use my institutionalised power and create change; if only to contain the fear teachers experience before and during an inspection. By airing these questions and opening up honest dialogue I would like to, 'Open the gap and insert the contradiction.'

Life has taught me that, along with having dreams and aspirations, you need to have a modicum of common sense and look at what it is humanly possible to achieve. In spite of contrary beliefs, I have seen many schools improve as a result of inspection. I have had the opportunity to work with many very skilled, highly enlightened human beings, who just as many drama practitioners that I know, have the child's interest at heart. Every child is entitled to the best possible education and whilst the present system may be flawed, it does highlight objectively areas that can be reassessed by schools so that the quality of education which is offered to children can be improved. The National Curriculum is not a strait-jacket. Teachers are perfectly at their leisure to develop their practice to teach subjects creatively and indeed must be encouraged to do so.

However, this innovative practice should not be hidden under a bushel. As drama teachers, we need to demystify our current modus operandi and come out of the closet by providing workshops for governors, senior management, parents and the local community which the school serves. We need to bring our documentation in line with Ofsted nomenclature so that inspectors can understand our aims, objectives, teaching styles and methodologies. Creating 'inexplicable mythologies' about our practice, known only by the circles we move in does not help our cause. We need to be able to offer clear explanations as to why working in the art form contributes to a humanised curriculum.

Our drama policies, schemes of work, long, medium and short term planning need to have clearly defined learning objectives, assessment opportunities and criteria for judging progress. We need to be able to clearly identify the knowledge, skills and understanding that pupils gain in drama lessons. I do not intend to open up the discussion in this article about the concept of opposition to the notion of Ofsted. Whilst this might be stimulating reading I do not think that this is what teachers require at this point in time. Teachers need practical suggestions as to what can help them in their preparation for Ofsted; how their subject fits into the inspection process, and the contribution that drama makes to the school provision of quality experiences which, if properly tracked and evaluated, can make a significant contribution to standards of attainment.

So where do we start?

The very first thing that the drama teacher needs to know is how to identify drama in relation to the school's aims and mission statement, and decide upon the ways that drama can contribute in putting these aims into practice (school ethos). See figure 1 for an example of this [The school aims are in the boxes].

Having established how drama ties in with the school aims, it is necessary to take a closer look at the requirements of the Ofsted framework and highlight the criteria which will contribute to the judgements the inspection team will make about the school. The published report must contain judgements on the following:

- The educational standards achieved.
- The quality of education provided.
- The spiritual, moral, social and cultural development of pupils.
- The effectiveness of the management of resources and finances.

The report must clearly state what does and does not work in the school and the subsequent impact that this has on the educational standards attained by the pupils. Although the inspection report must be written following certain criteria it is very important to remember that the school aims must be seen to be filtering through not only in the documentation of the school but also in the reality of the classroom. An attempt to show how this is achieved through drama can be traced in the chart following (see Figure 1). I hasten to add that this is a very crude interpretation and should only be used as a trigger for individual interpretation.

Having placed drama in the context of the school's aims let us now examine more closely the practical contribution drama can make to the implementation of these aims through the practice in the classroom which, hopefully, in turn, will be reflected in the process of inspection. The drama department needs to consider the ways in which drama contributes to the school's PROVISION, which in turn is linked to the school's OUTCOMES. These are discussed in greater detail later on.

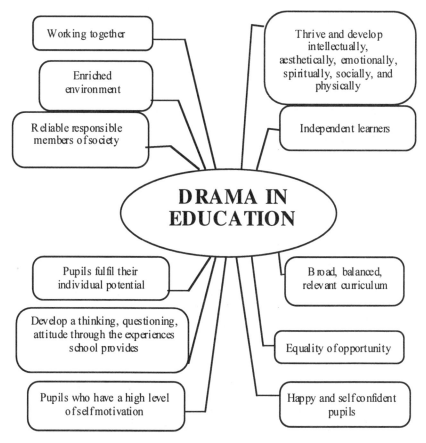

Figure 1   Drama in relation to the school's aims

For the benefit of the reader I have used different fonts for the areas of the school aims, the contribution of drama, and Ofsted requirements.

The aims of the school are :

To provide a broad, relevant and balanced curriculum   School

Drama makes a valuable contribution to understanding and interpreting of knowledge as defined by the National Curriculum but it also augments the National Curriculum requirements by its own body of knowledge based on theatre, culture, and pupils' life experiences.   *Drama*

Can be tracked through:

5.1	Teaching	Ofsted
5.2	Curriculum and Assessment	
5.3	Spiritual, moral, social, and cultural development	
6.1	Leadership and Management	

To have equality of opportunity   School

*All pupils have access to the curriculum and respond to it   Drama
through their personal meaning making.*

Can be traced through:

5.1	Teaching	Ofsted
5.2	Curriculum and Assessment	

To have happy and self confident pupils   School

*The transference of skills learnt in drama where pupils have   Drama
succeeded, can be applied to other areas of the curriculum
and to life in general. There is no failure, only different
levels of success through drama.*

Can be tracked through:

4.2	Attitudes, behaviour and personal development	Ofsted
5.3	Spiritual, moral, social, and cultural development	
5.4	Support, guidance and pupils' welfare	
5.5	Partnership with parents and the community	

To create reliable, responsible members of   School
society

*Drama has its own in-built system for 'rigour', based upon   Drama
precision, accuracy, and control. Working in a social art
form enables pupils to develop skills of empathy and multi
perspectives on social problems.*

Can be traced through:

4.1	Attainment and Progress	Ofsted
4.2	Attitudes, behaviour and personal development	
4.3	Attendance	
5.1	Teaching	
5.3	Spiritual, moral, social and cultural development	
5.5	Partnership with parents and the community	

To allow pupils to fulfil their individual potential   School

Drama is a legitimised vehicle for valuing imagination,   *Drama*
creativity and personal perception. Drama has its own built
in mechanism for differentiation.

Can be traced trough:

4.1   Attainment and progress   Ofsted
4.2   Attitudes, behaviour and personal development
5.1   Teaching
5.2   Curriculum and assessment

To allow pupils to thrive and develop   School intellectually, aesthetically, emotionally, spiritually, socially and physically

Drama is the holding form within which these areas can be   *Drama*
simultaneously developed through opportunities which are
provided for the pupils requiring a cognitive and affective
engagement with the process.

Can be traced through:

4.1   Attainment and progress   Ofsted
4.2   Attitudes, behaviour and personal development.
5.1   Teaching
5.3   Spiritual, moral, social and cultural development

To promote independent learners   School

Drama provides the opportunity for pupils to shape their   *Drama*
work by identifying a problem, investigating possible
solutions, deciding on the most appropriate solution,
testing that solution, appraising the effectiveness of that
solution, and identifying other directions and possible ways
forward.

Can be traced through:

4.1   Attainment and progress   Ofsted
4.2   Attitudes, behaviour and personal development
5.1   Teaching
5.2   Curriculum and assessment

To develop a thinking, questioning, attitude through the experiences the school provides

School

Drama encourages the development of a self-spectator by establishing unique opportunities for duality of experience:

Drama

Metaxis, "It is happening to me, I am making it happen."

Through reflection at the end of the lesson standards of attainment can be raised through personal desire, not external pressure.

Can be traced trough:

4.1   Attainment and progress

Ofsted

4.2   Attitudes, behaviour and personal development
5.3   Spiritual, moral, social and cultural development

To promote a high level of self-motivation

School

Drama breeds instant success as pupils become engaged with the material. Through skilled teacher intervention (Teacher as playwright, director), pupils become empowered and contribute to collective art making. (They can be led from unconscious incompetence to conscious competence).

Drama

Can be traced through:

4.2   Attitudes, behaviour and personal development

Ofsted

5.1   Teaching

To promote co-operative working

School

Drama is a social art form which promotes collaborative skills. The teaching paradigm is 'child as crucible' (you and I keep stirring things around). The teaching style is interactive, dynamic.

Drama

Can be traced through:

4.1   Attainment and progress

Ofsted

4.2   Attitudes, behaviour and personal development
5.1   Teaching
5.3   Spiritual, moral, social, and cultural development
5.4   Support, guidance and pupils' welfare
5.5   Partnership with parents and the community

102

To create an enriched environment   **School**

Drama is a balance of teacher and pupil expertise, cognitive,   Drama
affective, and contemporary knowledge which presents
knowledge in a variety of forms.

Can be traced through:

5.1   Teaching   Ofsted
5.2   Curriculum and assessment
5.3   Spiritual, moral, social, and cultural development

Having placed drama in relation to the school aims, I now wish to explore
its contribution to the wider context of the Ofsted inspection. The following chart
denotes the structure of the inspection, and the areas on which judgements will be
made and will contribute to the final report.

Structure of Inspection

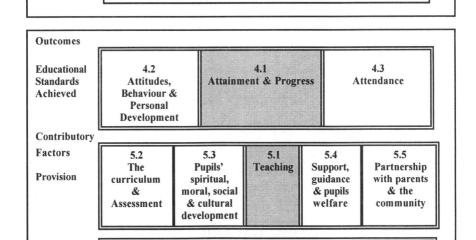

I will discuss in greater detail each aspect of the structure of the inspection
and make recommendations for the drama co-ordinator (subjects are obviously

reported upon separately in the report).

So how can the drama teacher / co-ordinator best prepare for the inspection? I shall look at each aspect of the framework separately and offer practical suggestions as to what is required and what evidence can be collected. The most important point to remember is that Drama is a part of the school's **provision**, related to the quality of education that it provides for its pupils, and, if carefully monitored by the drama teacher / co-ordinator, evidence can be found of the impact of this **provision** on the school's **outcomes**, (standards, behaviour etc.). See chart entitled '**Structure of Inspection**'.

3.1   Characteristics of the school

In this section, Inspectors need to know what is pupils' attainment on entry. Dorothy Heathcote's phrase "the social health of the class" is worth commenting on in the documentation.

- Have pupils ever experienced drama before?
- What is the social emotional and academic background pupils bring with them?
- What is the catchment area of the school?
- What is the ethnic mix?
- Are there high levels of unemployment?
- What is the nature of the pupils' speaking and listening skills?

⇒ [These factors are very important! Inspectors will take account of this information when making judgements about progress in relation to pupils' prior attainment.]

4.1   Attainment and progress

Under this heading, evidence is gathered about standards in subjects. This evidence is gathered from lesson observation and from pupil interviews; teachers' plans and assessments are scrutinised and judgements are made about academic standards.

- What do pupils know and understand?
- What standards are they attaining?
- Can they build belief, sustain a role, create productive tension etc.?
- How much progress do they make in a lesson?
- How much progress do they make over a period of time?
- How do they use literacy, numeracy and I.T. competencies in lessons?
- What are the standards of SEN pupils?
- Are there differences in attainment between boys and girls?
- Do pupils take initiatives, or are they teacher dependent?
- Do pupils learn from mistakes and do they apply this knowledge to new situations?
- What do the pupils know about the art form of drama, cultural developments in drama, famous playwrights, the elements of play making etc.?

- What contributions does drama make to the wider community?

4.2 Attitudes, behaviour and personal development

Lesson observations and behaviour around the school will form the basis for evidence gathering. In lessons inspectors will look at the following areas;

- How do pupils co-operate and behave in the drama lesson?
- Are they offered challenges and degrees of independence?
- Are they able to sustain concentration?
- Do they show respect for the subject?
- Are relationships constructive?
- Do pupils show respect for other people's feelings, viewpoints, ideas, values and beliefs?
- Are teachers' strategies for behaviour management effective?
- Are pupils able to defer their own self gratification for the benefit of the group in order to move the drama forward?

4.3 Attendance

Evidence is gathered about the impact attendance rates have on standards. Inspectors will be looking at whether:

- Lessons start on time.
- There are adequate systems in place to detect truancy.
- Parents are informed about pupils' lateness.
- Does late registration detract from time allocated to drama?

5.1 Teaching

Inspectors observe lessons, making judgements on the following criteria related to teaching:

- Secure subject knowledge.
- High expectations.
- Use of questioning and challenges set.
- Knowledge of pupils' needs.
- Quality of lesson planning.
- Clear learning objectives.
- Extension activities.
- Use of exposition.
- Checking of pupils' understanding.
- Pace and use of time.
- Use, quality and range of assessments.
- Homework.
- Classroom organisation.
- Quality of relationships.
- Behaviour management.
- Use of praise.
- Quality and use of resources.
- Use of support staff, parents.

- Strengths and weaknesses in teaching.

5.2   The curriculum and assessment

Inspectors will interview co-ordinators and read documentation provided by the department in order to gain evidence on the school's provision in this area.

- Is appropriate time allocated to the subject?
- Is the drama curriculum broad and balanced?
- Does drama promote pupils' intellectual and aesthetic development?
- Is there equality of access for all pupils?
- Does the drama curriculum contribute to SEN pupils' individual education plans?
- Is the long, medium, short term planning clear and effective?
- Does it provide continuity and progression of learning?
- Is there extra curricular provision? e.g. drama club.
- Are there visits to the theatre?
- Are assessments used to inform planning?
- Does the school encourage the use of TIE companies?
- Are pupils' achievements in drama logged in their personal portfolios?
- Are drama records informative?
- Do parents understand what is happening in drama?
- Does drama have an impact on standards in other subjects?

5.3   Pupils' spiritual, moral, social, and cultural development

Inspectors will scrutinise documentation, interview teachers, look at evidence from displays and talk to pupils.

- Is there evidence of awe and wonder? Is there an element of spirituality in drama?
- How does drama contribute to pupils' personal, moral, social and cultural development?
- Are opportunities provided for recognition of contributions from great theatre practitioners of different cultures?
- Are emotive responses explained and developed?
- Are pupils encouraged to develop and explore a strong moral code?
- What is the quality of relationships in co-operative ways of working?
- What examples are set by adults in the school?
- Are SEN pupils encouraged?
- Are broader cultural issues addressed?
- Are opportunities provided to appreciate different cultural heritages?
- Are gender issues explored?

5.4   Support, guidance and pupils' welfare

This evidence is gathered from governors, pastoral care, interviews & lesson observations.

- How well do staff support pupils' needs?

- Do pupils have opportunities to express their opinions?
- Do pupils receive advice on academic progress and personal development?
- Are they encouraged to make comments?
- Does the school have effective procedures for child protection?

5.5   Partnership with parents and the community
This evidence is gathered from examining the parents' questionnaire, interviews with parents and detailed analyses of the school prospectus.
- Do parents have a clear line of communication?
- Do they help in classrooms?
- Is their expertise used across the school?
- Does the school or drama department encourage an audit of parental expertise?
- What is the quality of information that is provided for the parents?
- What links are there with the local community?
- Do these links impact on pupils' attainment?

6.1   Leadership and management
This evidence is mostly gained from documentation and interviews with SMT and subject co-ordinators.
- How is the subject co-ordinated throughout the school?
- Has the co-ordinator been on recent and relevant courses?
- Has any amount of money, which has been spent on the department, (resources, books, tapes, etc.) had an impact on standards?
- What is the degree and quality of dialogue between teachers in relation to drama?
- Is drama taught as a subject or as a method?
- Is the scheme of work clear and purposeful?
- Are governors aware of what is being taught?
- Does drama contribute to other areas of the curriculum?
- Is there any evidence that the skills and knowledge taught through drama are applied to other subjects. (A tracking audit is a useful way of checking this out and, obviously, asking the pupils as to whether their thinking skills have improved).
- Does the co-ordinator assess regularly and are these assessments used to inform future planning?
- Are workshops provided for parents and governors?
- Are inter-school cluster groups established?
- Are support staff involved in the planning of drama lessons?
- Do they know what is going on?

6.2   Staffing, accommodation and learning resources
Inspectors will look for evidence to see if this area has an effect on standards
- Are the teachers appropriately qualified to teach drama?

- Do they work effectively as a team?
- Have they got clear job descriptions?
- Do staff plan together?
- Are appropriate courses attended?
- Is drama on the school development plan?
- How well are new teachers inducted into the drama department?
- What is the nature and level of support given to them?
- Is teacher appraisal in line with requirements?
- Are drama teachers' professional needs considered?
- Is the accommodation adequate?
- Are the physical needs of SEN pupils taken into consideration?
- Are resources adequate?
- Do they have an impact on standards?
- Does the library contain books on theatre, stage craft, drama?

6.3   The efficiency of the school

This is a crucial area for making judgements on whether the school provides good, sound or poor value for money. Inspectors evaluate:

- The money spent on staff, resources, training etc. and the impact that this has on standards of attainment.
- Standards are compared to financial output, i.e. if £2,500 was spent on training courses for the drama department, what impact has it had on standards?
- Do governors evaluate major financial spending?
- Is there efficient financial control and school administration?
- Does the school provide vale for money in forms of educational standards achieved and quality of education provided in relation to its context and income?

I have tried to explain the rather complicated process of inspections in relation to drama in education. This can not be viewed as a mechanistic 'tick sheet' as it is much more complicated than that, and it requires corporate team judgements. I hasten to add that this paper is a subjective view on an objective framework. I have attempted to deconstruct the requirements in order to meet the needs of drama teachers. I am more than happy to enter into professional dialogue with colleagues who require further amplification on the framework, under the auspices of NATD.

Thank you to all of my drama colleagues who have helped me on my journey so far.

I would also ask readers not to reproduce any of this documentation, without my, (the author's) prior permission, as I have a long way to go in concretising my thinking.

Notes

1. Neurolinguistic Programming: Harry Adler Piatkus 1994 : p. 22.

Humanising GCSE

Guy Williams

Guy Williams is Head of Drama at Josiah Mason Sixth Form College, Birmingham.

Introduction

In 1987, GCSEs were introduced. Ostensibly this was to do away with the two tier system of examination at 16+, providing a universal marker that everyone could understand. Under the old system, 'O' levels were considered to be for the more able and CSEs for the less able. At 'O' level, grades A - E represented a pass. At CSE, a grade 1 was considered to be the equivalent of an 'O' level pass. For GCSE it was said that the grades A - G would all be considered as passes. However, A - C are still considered to be the acceptable grades to achieve, and indeed in many subjects there are graded papers so that some young people will not be able to achieve the top grades.

I mention this as background because it touches on one of the central concerns of the conference which seemed to me to be polarised around: accommodation or collusion. This was most clear in the debate over ERA (Educational Reform Act) and Ofsted: do we continue to fight for the repeal of the act or do we work from within for change?

GCSEs fall right in the centre of the debate. Historically they are of ERA. The double talk and deceit that surrounded their rushed introduction still angers some. The Government response of 'What are you complaining about? This is what teachers have been asking for years,' typified the ruthless steamrollering of legislation that was to become their hallmark. It has led to a desperately impoverished curriculum and increasingly savage attacks on both teachers and young people alike.

The workshops at the conference sought to address these concerns. On one level, the whole notion of examinations is abhorrent: filling young people into a normal curve of distribution; 'assessing' their ability in a particular area of knowledge on a couple of summer days; actually only testing their short term memory in many instances. On another, the kind of tests that are currently being devised are clearly culturally specific and Euro-centric; alienate many by their lack of relevance; are so narrow that the level of competence they claim to assess is doubtful anyway; and in a climate of league tables and the threat of payment by results, there is much evidence of teaching to the tests rather than the needs of the young people.

But that debate was for another time and place. What was at issue here was:
- given that we are working within a system which examines young people's abilities at 16, how can we best meet their needs?

- how can we create a humanising curriculum which enables all young people to realise their full potential?

The first question to be addressed through the workshops examined the choice of syllabuses:
- 'do the objectives and marking criteria allow me as Teacher/Guardian to facilitate the full development of the young people with whom I have the privilege to work?'

In other words, does the choice of syllabus affect the quality of the education that can be provided?

The second question addressed the factors that led to decisions as to which syllabus should be chosen by scrutinising the detail:
- 'how can the structures offered by the syllabus be used to enable an approach which is humanising and child-centred?'

In other words, what kind of teaching and learning will take place if I work through these structures?

We have to decide first what kind of education we need to provide for young people and then to find the system which enables us to do this.

The workshops
The work of the weekend seeks to bring together a number of strands through practical work.

Running parallel are three key elements:
1) The text of Titus Andronicus;
2) The frame of theatre workers preparing to take the play to Bosnia;
3) Teachers exploring GCSE structures.

Central to all three is the question:

'What are the responsibilities of the Guardians in the development of the child?'

1)TITUS ANDRONICUS
Extracts used:
Act I Scene i lines 79 - 89
Act I Scene i lines 276 - 298
Act III Scene i lines 4 - 11
Act V Scene iii lines 35 - 46

The extracts focus on Titus' treatment of his offspring.

2)　As theatre workers preparing to take the piece to Bosnia, the participants are invited to bring two qualities to the play:

- the perspective of an audience whose perception might be more direct than a British one;
- the conscious manipulation of the Theatre form to reveal the dramatic action of the play.

3)　As teachers, they are invited to scrutinise the GCSE syllabuses offered by MEG, SEG and ULEAC. In order to address the central question, they are invited to ask:

- do the objectives and marking criteria allow me as Teacher/Guardian to facilitate the full development of the young people with whom I have the privilege to work?
- how can the structures offered by the syllabus be used to enable an approach which is humanising and child-centred?

Dear Mr Williams

I have pleasure in inviting you to bring your version of Titus Andronicus to the 18th International Theatre Festival this summer.
1 have enclosed a slide to show you your performance venue, the cave that you requested and a plan of it to help you with your set design. I have also included a few images of Mostar today - all of them from the East side of course. You should also know that temperatures during the day are normally in the mid 30s Centigrade and 45°C is quite normal. Please bear this in mind in your planning.
Please fax your set design to us as soon as possible so that we can start gathering the materials for building it.
Also, publicity needs to be sent so that we can start advertising it for you.
If you wish to have material included in a programme, we need to have that as soon as possible so that we can translate and print it in time for your first performance.

With the best regards

Art Director of MTM
Sead Dulic

MOSTARSKI TEATAR MLADIH,　A　Bitange　18　88000 MOSTAR BOSNA I HERCEGOVINA. TEUFAX: + 387(0) 8855 11 99

Figure 1　　　　Letter from Sead Dulic (MTM)

KEY TO CAVE PLAN

a) Raised area approx. 2 m above cave floor

b) Large rock in middle of cave with elephant carved on front

c) Apron (cave floor)

d) Raked seating

Note:
At its highest point the roof of the cave is approx. 9 m high. The roof slopes down so that its is only 3 m above head height at point *a*.

Tasks
1)   Create parsimonious working notebook.

2)   Identify the syllabus they want to explore.

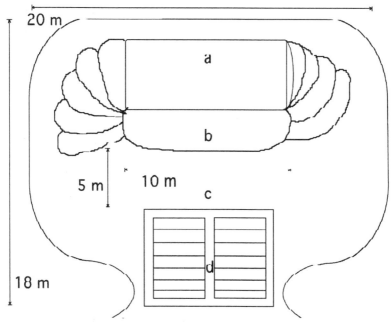

Figure 2   Plan of the Cave

3)   Building belief in the Frame:
            Three photographs of the awards ceremony they recently attended;

Office noticeboard;
Name and logo of company.

4)   Company meeting setting the main task: letter from Sead Dulic (see Figure 1). Imply previous discussion; letter is confirmation; identify initial roles.

5)   Explore material sent: photographs, slides (if possible), plan of cave (see Figure 2), books.

6)   Notebook reflection: journal entry of theatre worker anticipating problems for the role.

7)   Extract 1: Titus buries his sons.
    a)   Before leaving to do battle with the Goths, Titus receives his sons.
        •   Each member of the Company is one of his 25 sons (Lucius, Martius, Quintus, Mutius and their 21 un-named brothers).
        •   Facilitator takes role of Titus. Shape Titus.
        •   Group depiction of the meeting.
        •   Who is prepared to speak? What would they say?
        •   What are they thinking?
        •   What significant object do they have about them that reveals their relationship to their father?
    b)   'Father returns home'.
        •   Depiction of extract 1.
    c)   Company decide how the extract will be performed in the final production.

8)   Notebook reflection: journal entry, the final diary entry that Titus' son makes before going into battle against the Goths.

9)   Set design. Clearly the tomb is significant. 'Ad Manes Fratrum', 'To the spirits of our brothers' is inscribed above the entrance: the company offer designs for the tomb and build it. (Sugar paper, newspaper, cloth, gaffa tape available).
        Plan to be faxed to MTM.

10)   Notebook reflection: notes towards set design: how does this enable the audience to understand the central question?

11)   Extract 2: Titus kills his son, Mutius.
    a)   Participant playing Mutius offers her/his object.

        Create three moments from the past relationship with his father:
            i)   the moment of his birth;
            ii)   the first time Mutius remembers his father being proud of him;

iii)   the night before the first battle.

b)   Create the physical map of the extract (ref. Stanislavski's method of physical action).
Speak the objectives of each character: 'I want ... '
Improvise the extract in action only.

c)   The company decide how the extract will be performed in the final performance.

12)   Notebook reflection: what your character would like to have said and done at the moment of the death of Mutius.

13)   NATD reflection: return to the central question: what are our initial thoughts in each of the three strands?

14)   Extract 3: Titus weeps and begs for the release of his sons Quintus and Martius.
a)   Shape Company member as Titus/Guardian.
Company take up attitude which reveals in depiction and one sentence the factors that have shaped Titus.

b)   The Company decide how the extract will be performed in the final performance.

15)   Notebook reflection: poster design.

16)   In pairs, offer costume design for one character. Use newspaper and cloths. Company decide design that most effectively helps the play.

17)   Notebook reflection: design: how does this help the audience understand the central question?

18)   Extract 4: Titus kills his daughter, Lavinia.
a)   Company sculpt Lavinia.
Attach labels to her which describe her Father's attitude towards her.
Sculpt Titus at the moment after Lavinia's death.
Attach labels which describe how society now sees him.

b)   Company decide how the extract will be performed in the final production.

19)   Notebook reflection: Programme notes.

20)   Return to original syllabus groups. Answer questions.

21)   Return to central question.

The New Drama 'A' Level

Pauline Marson

Pauline Marson is Deputy Head at Henbury School, Bristol, and co-devisor of the new drama 'A' level.

Many of us have long wanted another choice for Post-16 students in Drama. Working with colleagues we have shaped Post 16 A and A/S level which builds on the terrific achievements of students and teachers in the earlier key stages.

The aim was always to set out a syllabus in <u>Drama,</u> one that would encompass all that the subject means, but retain a philosophical whole and possess a coherence which could be experienced by candidates. Courses designed to fulfil this syllabus invite students to make links between the different elements which are of necessity interconnected.

Paper 1
Devising
Drama
2 Group
devised pieces

Paper 2
Exploration
through
Drama
Teacher- tech
Consideration
of 2 areas of
drama

Paper 4
Understanding
Drama
includes
analysis
preview and a
creative
question

Paper 3
Text in
Performance
coherent group
performance

Course work: teacher assessed   Externally examined

Paper		A/S	A
	1 20%	1 devised piece	2 devised pieces
	2 20%	1 scheme	2 schemes
	3 30%	1 performance	1 performance
	4 30%	2 questions	3 questions

There is no prescribed content: drama is too immediate, vibrant and comprehensive to be summed up in set texts or practitioners who represent a genre which may not reflect the needs of the candidates, or the best work available currently for them to see.

The opportunity to look at world drama - not all of which is scripted, to consider how women, for example, have shaped trends in drama as practitioners and to design a course where the activities which come naturally in a Drama setting in education, has been welcomed by teachers.

The course looked at the philosophy of the syllabus as a whole, then addressed each paper in turn, supplying teachers with strategies for teaching the syllabus and enabling colleagues to share experiences.

Aims of the session at the conference
To introduce the new 'A' level syllabus.
To enable teachers to plan activities for their own students.
To consider the holistic nature of drama.
To work as practitioners, critics, interpreters and creators of drama at our own level.

Sessions 1 and 2
A new 'A' Level Drama was needed to enable other progression routes from GCSE. Our aim was to produce a coherent syllabus, with an emphasis on teaching rather than on a prescribed body of knowledge. An A/S course was very attractive to schools and students. The very act of introducing alternative Post-16 courses alongside Dearing's review, has led to a general improvement in syllabuses on offer.

Working as a group, the challenge was to prove that the links were implicit and explicit within a course designed to lead to A/AS level Drama.

We started by using a stimulus, Susan Packer's photograph of a baby surrounded by toys, but not engaging with the environment, set for the 1997 written exam, but using it, as you might in teaching, as a resource for devising drama. We identified two threads, which are a feature of the new 'A' level

- themes and issues
- style and genre

Two groups showed their creative work. One looked at expectations and labelling, using a circle to lift a baby (crumpled up flip chart paper) and pass around each member, who set out a life for the child. The other group re-created the picture, allowing us to see how love cannot be passed on through material things. Assessment methods and processes were explained.

We then looked at a sample scheme of work with the theme of 'Protest', which included the study of how Brecht, Wertenbaker and Wolfe presented questions about protest to an audience using different genres. This is a sample Paper 2 Exploration scheme and was used to relate to the opening scene of 'The Caucasian Chalk Circle'.

Sessions 3 and 4

Study of text does not have to start with the text. Over lunch, the room was arranged with a tight circle of chairs within which lay the baby, and two council tables. Who knows what is best for our valley? Two observers watched out for dramatic moments, whilst two messengers attempted to set up communications between the two groups.

The role play began with members working fully committedly in role.

> *"Now that the troubles are over ... you wish to return to farming in this fertile valley. Your houses overlook the river, it is your green and pleasant land.*
>
> *There are the others, 'them' who risked a great deal during the times you were evacuated, fighting for the valley. They may wish to remain here.*

Prepare your plans.

As Brecht knew, the only way to resolve this conflict is to see a play.
We reviewed the learning about Brecht that arose from the experience and identified techniques actors might use in lifting words from the page, before rehearsing scene 1 of the play.

Observers had noted techniques which were Brechtian in style in the role play, as well as thematic links with Cyprus, the Gaza Strip and Northern Ireland. Some examples were:-

Ceremony
Eye contact of messenger
Intense <u>attitude</u> of listening - three levels   -   *observers*
                                                        -   *messengers*
                                                        -   *participants*

Actors have views
Persuasive language/tone
Vocabulary of respect

We need a play to resolve this!

We then turned to look at the 'struggle for the valley' in the Caucasian Chalk Circle.

The session ended in sharing: sharing the drama work of the groups, the ideas arising from the stimulus.

Ideas for Paper 1 from the group

Paper 1

Blake 'The Smile'
Heaney 'Rattlebag/School bag'
  'My parents kept me from children who were rough ...'
'Sheets'

Ideas for Paper 2 from the group

Paper 2

Beckett/Bond - 'Saved'.
South Africa/Protest Theatre.
Saved - E. Bond Social Realism - Teaching morals/ethics
Joan Littlewood's work.

Colleagues enjoyed the experience, found it stimulating and stretching, and that is just what we hope for in our Post-16 students.

The Meeting Point Between Drama and Text: Thoughts from a Workshop

Fiona Lesley

Fiona Lesley is the education officer for English Touring Theatre.

Introduction

The following commentary and suggestions focus on an exploration of Chekhov's *The Seagull* as a valuable drama resource when working with young people. The workshop which took place at the conference drew from experiences in working with students across the country alongside English Touring Theatre's production of the play. I would like to acknowledge the invaluable contribution of Susanna Harding who led and devised the original programme with me and to thank the creative team and acting company of the production whose work informed the education programme.

Chekhov's work has become shrouded in a veil of inaccessibility and high brow theory which denies the exacting nature of his examination of human behaviour and its radical provocation to our own understanding of the relationship between the individual and the world. Whilst the play details a very particular set of experiences socially and historically, it presents a tension between the idealism of youthful ambition and the cruel realities of an adult world which challenges fundamental perceptions of how our journeys through life are made.

The workshop

In seeking to approach the play with a respect for Chekhov's clarity and equanimity in his presentation of human behaviour, the workshop focused on the play as a powerful exposition of the fundamental dynamics of drama. This emphasis combined a rigorous approach to analysis of the text with increasing participants' awareness of their own personal qualities in performance work and drama exercises. Drawing these two strands together and weaving an increasingly detailed approach to critical analysis with a growing sense of personal spirit, the workshop aimed to develop participants' understanding of their own 'make-up' in response to the play's examination of the individual in society. Whilst the characters in Chekhov's plays are not subject to influences which can be directly applied to everyone's experience, his dramatic technique belies a powerful exposure of the dynamics of personal development.

In seeking to unravel the mystery of individual 'essence' which is often suggested as a goal in performing naturalistic texts, the workshop focused on human energy as a tangible force in life and performance which can be examined, developed, harnessed and changed. Using this focus, the workshop embraced the power of our individual spirits as the manifestation of our particular journeys simultaneously escaping definition even as it distinguishes us from each other. In working with students on aspects of human energy, a vivid and dynamic force can be released which encompasses a truth to individual experience whilst constantly raising awareness of behaviour and the manifestations of our particular prejudices.

The exercises

As this document is being compiled to enable teachers to use and draw on the work that took place at the conference, it seems important to try and describe or outline the stages of the process. Whilst all the actual techniques are relatively straightforward they may appear strange out of their practical context and without the relevant excerpts from the text. However, they may also remind people of exercises they have used and forgotten about and can be picked up and applied to each teacher's personal approach.

I - Warm-up

'Pass The Energy' (Pass the clap!) - to begin as a group to identify this notion of energy as a force that can be examined and developed - simply pass energy round a circle by making a clap. No need to register receiving, simply pass on or back. No passing across the circle. This apparently simple exercise can be 'achieved' quite quickly. The emphasis here should be on developing the game until everyone can 'see' the energy. It is not being used here simply as a means of developing concentration.

'A Day In Your Life' - ask the participants to find a place on the floor on their own. They are to think of a day of the week, not any particular day when such and such happened, just a usual Monday/Tuesday etc. The facilitator will call out various times of the day when participants will begin acting out whatever they usually do at this time. Simply ask the group to be aware of their own energy and how it manifests itself. It is important not to make this about mime or originality but to focus on just doing. Go through the times from morning to night, about 4 examples, and then repeat the exercise but this time ask the participants to have a preoccupation. Something is on their mind. Look at examples and discuss levels of energy, energy shifts and base energies.

II - Preparation

'What is being expressed' - divide the group into small groups of 3-5 and give them a list of excerpts from the text where key characters talk about themselves. Ask the group to summarise what is being expressed in each quotation. One person in the group takes notes. They divide a sheet of paper into 4 columns headed: FACT, FEELING, HEAD and HEART. Any group will have to work hard to try to identify what is being **expressed** without invoking a generalised judgment of the character. The idea is to try to understand the energy behind the words and to consider whether it is factual information (fact), an emotional moment (feeling), an expression of how they have analysed their own experience (head), or a deep-felt commitment to something (heart).

III - Individual work

Ask each participant to work on their own and to consider what they have discovered about the character they have looked at. You may use visualisation or any other form of imaginative stimulus. Ask them to consider how the information they have would manifest itself in the energy of the character;

Physically - What effect would their particular physical circumstances have on their posture ....?

Emotionally - Where would any tensions be located ... ?

Intellectually - How would the way they interpret their experience affect their stature?
Finally, how would their deep felt concerns manifest themselves; what would this person 'bring into a room'?

Ask each participant to choose a line from the excerpts they have looked at and to move about in the space and deliver the line. This work can be developed in whatever way is most appropriate for the group. It should lead to a close analysis of behaviour and how our influences and responses to them are made manifest in constantly **shifting energy**.

IV - Interaction

Return to the groups who worked on analysing the excerpts. Give each group a list of lines other characters say about 'their' character. Ask one person to be in the centre of a circle with the energy they found for their character. The people forming the circle spontaneously read lines from the sheets trying to colour their tone with the various characters' attitudes. The person in the centre simply responds physically to what they hear. They may ignore some comments and warm to others, etc. The rest of the participants watch the exercise and feed back to the group about how they noticed this character reacts and deals with the world.

V - Moments of reflection

Staying in your character groups, give each group an excerpt from the text where the character talks about a moment in their past. First ask the group to create the moment that is described. This can be done in whatever way suits your group but it is quite likely that it will have a surreal quality because it is a moment of reflection. You may choose to enhance this by focusing on sound, often the most vivid sensory trigger in memory. Whatever guidelines you give you should include a moment of focus where the protagonist (the character whose memory it is) makes an action which expresses his or her response to the experience. Then, working in pairs, return to the moment where the reflection takes place. This is where their past (head), as they choose to interpret it, is brought into their present (feeling) and touches some aspect of yearning for the future (heart). In pairs, find the trigger which brings the memory into active contact with that character's desires for the future.

VI - Scene work

All of these elements can be brought together in looking at a moment from a scene. This should include work on the **dynamics** of the scene by using improvisation and exercises which use the manifestation of energy to impact action.

Conclusion

By using this balance between instinctive approaches to experience and critical analysis of human behaviour, we can generate a warmth and generosity in how we approach each other which is also based on sharpening our skills in analysis, observation and understanding. Chekhov's writing invokes a highly detailed and complex understanding of human behaviour. By respecting the radical spirit of his approach to experience we can understand the significance of our own journeys, be observant about the role we play in building our own 'character' and have some power to change it through a better awareness of our own energy and individuality.

First Encounters with *Alchemy*
and
Queer Goings-On in *The Cherry Orchard*

Brian Woolland

Brian Woolland is a senior lecturer in Drama and Education at the University of Reading.

The Saturday workshops

Ben Jonson: first encounters with Alchemy

In the television show *Have I Got News for You,* one of the rounds involves the teams looking at a group of pictures; and guessing which is 'the odd one out'. You know the kind of thing: Ben Jonson, Peter Barnes, Charles Dickens, Edward Bond, John Arden[1]. There are always several likely answers (Charles Dickens because he wrote novels and the others are playwrights; John Arden because he lives in Ireland and the others live(d) in England ...) but no - the 'right' answer is never the obvious one: Angus Deayton (the quiz master) is annoyingly revealed as the fount of arcane wisdom. But then Paul Merton always mocks the very idea of the closed question, and everything's alright - after all, even if his suggestions don't get rewarded with points, he gets the best laughs; and that's what really matters ...

I wonder how many of the children we teach go through school either submitting to the determined correctness of their teachers and examiners or learning to survive by mocking them. As drama teachers, many of us know how rewarding it can be for a child/student to be able to entertain their peers by entertainingly subverting the system.

As drama teachers, we pride ourselves on being able to work <u>with</u> our students for much of the time; we try <u>not</u> to have all the answers, we try to create situations which demand collaborative responses. But when it comes to teaching plays the problem rears its head again: how to overcome the intimidation of the text; how to counteract the sense (often encouraged by teachers) that there is a 'right' way of reading the text, that its meanings exist before each new audience approaches it.

One of the implications of this notion that each text has pre-existent meanings is that any audience is thereby constructed as culturally homogenous.

The workshops that I led at the NATD conference were designed primarily to address some of these issues. In particular I wanted to overcome the sense of intimidation that so frequently accompanies approaches to play texts.

There were many reasons for the specific choice of plays that we explored on the two days of the conference. I chose to explore *The Alchemist* (1610) because:

- Ben Jonson's work is frequently characterised as 'difficult' - and therefore especially intimidating. I wanted to work on a text that the participants were not likely to know, putting them in the same position that most of our students find themselves in.
- *The Alchemist* is in itself about theatre. Jonson teaches us about the nature of theatre, and questions many of the basic assumptions that we make.
- Jonson was probably the first English playwright to think about theatre as an educative medium; and to write about theatre in this way.
- The whole canon of Jonson's plays is grossly undervalued in England.

The approach adopted in the workshops was to set up possibilities for exploring, for finding out about the text, whilst never letting the workshop participants (for 5 of whom English was a second language) become intimidated by it. Equally, I did not want the workshop to be dominated by improvisatory work. I wanted the text itself to be of central importance; and for the workshops to OPEN UP possible meanings rather than *teaching* pre-existent meanings.

So my **aims** for the two days' workshops were simple:
1. to encourage an attitude of excited curiosity about *The Alchemist* and (in the Sunday workshop) Chekhov's *The Cherry Orchard*;
2. to explore the texts in such a way that they might reveal new insights both for the participants and for myself.

The **objectives** were that by the end of the day the workshop participants should -
1. have interrogated the play as actively as possible;
2. want to read (or re-read) *The Alchemist* and to see it (and other Jonson plays) performed in the theatre.

I have often wondered why Jonson is perceived to be so very 'difficult'. His critics claim that his language is complex and obscure, his plots are convoluted and his characterisation is thin. I would challenge all of these contentions. Each of them reveals an approach to the plays as literature rather than as theatre. My own assessment of why he has been 'written off' is precisely that his plays are so theatrical. I was very fortunate in <u>seeing</u> a Jonson before attempting to read any. And the more work that I've done, the more convinced I am that his work is extraordinarily 'modern'. What makes him so 'difficult' to read is that every character he creates has a 'voice'; he uses language playfully, but always actively; his plotting IS complicated, but it's tremendous fun and the characters grow out of Commedia style types. When I have worked on any of his

124

plays with students (from lower sixth to undergraduate level) I have found they quickly become enormously enthused by them.

The workshops

The following is a summary of the activities undertaken in each of the workshops - together with a brief explanation of their purpose.

1.   *The persons of the play*

SUBTLE	The Alchemist
FACE	The Housekeeper
DOLL COMMON	Their Colleague
DAPPER	A Clerk
DRUGGER	A Tobacco-man
LOVEWIT	The Master of the House
EPICURE MAMMON	A Knight
SURLY	A Gamester
TRIBULATION	A Pastor of Amsterdam
ANANIAS	A Deacon There
KASTRIL	The Angry Boy
DAME PLIANT	His Sister: a Widow

Working in small groups, participants are asked to look carefully at the list of characters (as above); and to use this information to speculate about the play. What do you associate with the names of each of the characters? What kind of play do you expect it to be if it has characters with names such as Face, Subtle, Dapper? Note down any questions you want to ask. Note down what you might expect from these characters. Keep the notes and refer back to them. These notes were written on OHP acetates, so that each group's speculations and questions could be shared with others. In our workshop a number of very interesting questions were raised: notably around the characters of **Face** and **Drugger**. One member of the group who spoke Italian noted that **Face** might be a reference to the Italian *Facia*, a word meaning mask. Given her perception of the characters as 'types' she also wanted to know what the relationship between this play and Commedia dell Arte might be. Several people thought **Drugger** (the tobacco man) might be the seventeenth century equivalent of a dealer. 'Is he as shady a character as he seems?' 'How does Jonson's language relate to ours?'

As a teacher, I tried to prioritise these questions, to focus the group's attention on specific questions as we worked through other material. And, as the teacher, I see it as very important that I do not contribute to the sense of intimidation. If the group feel that I always know more about the material than they do, they are likely to be limited in their response. If they ASK questions, if they want to know about the material, I will answer as best I can; but I need to limit the flow of information. My experience of the text is there for them to make use of. Above all I want to arouse curiosity; and keep it alive.

Had we had longer, I would have liked the small groups to attempt to show us examples of each of the characters' behaviour/physical mannerisms - always trying to keep the intelligent guesswork as active as possible.

2. *The Argument*

A teacher-led activity. Under the direction of the teacher, volunteers are used to enact Jonson's plot summary which precedes the text. Participants are then encouraged to note any further questions they have at this stage about the play; and to note whether any of their earlier questions have been 'answered' or whether the questions themselves need modifying.

THE ARGUMENT

> The sickness hot, a master quit, for fear,
> His house in town, and left one servant there.
> Ease him corrupted, and gave means to know
> A cheater and his punk; who, now brought low,
> Leaving their narrow practice, were become
> Coz'ners at large; and only wanting some
> House to set up, with him they here contract
> Each for a share, and all begin to act.
> Much company they draw, and much abuse,
> In casting figures, telling fortunes, news,
> Selling of flies, flat bawdy, with the stone;
> Till it, and they, and all in fume are gone.

3. *Characters and their 'voices'*

The playful interrogation of the text continues. In small groups (all our work was collaborative) people looked at a number of short extracts from the text. Each of these was chosen because it shed more light on a specific character. Look, for example at the extracts below:

Drugger arrives at 'The Alchemist's' wanting help. He explains to **Subtle**:

DRUGGER   ... I am a young beginner, and am building
> Of a new shop, and like your worship; just,
> At corner of a street: (Here's the plot on't.)
> And I would know, by art, sir, of your worship,
> Which way I should make my door, by necromancy.
> And where my shelves. And, which should be for boxes.
> And which for pots. I would be glad to thrive, sir.
> And, I was wished to your worship, by a gentleman,
> One Captain Face, that says you know men's planets,
> And their good angels and their bad.

Every punctuation mark here is a signifier of speech rhythm; every 'and' is indicative of Drugger's vocal mannerism.

The small groups were then asked to prepare a 'performance of Drugger's 'speech' with Subtle present. The groups were asked to make Subtle's silence an active agent in the piece. Every group's presentation was different. In one, Subtle stared at Drugger, listening intently but inscrutable; and Drugger became more and more nervous. In another he took little notice of Drugger, apparently concerning himself with an arcane text, and only occasionally looking up quizzically. The extract demonstrates Jonson's theatricality. Whatever the specific stage business, Subtle's silence is as important as Drugger's speech. In the workshops we looked at a number of other short extracts, in each case trying to find appropriate vocal mannerisms and speech rhythms through short practical exercises; and searching the short texts for indicators of action.

One more example: **Kastril** visits 'The Alchemist'. As you can tell from his accent, he's from out of town:

> **KASTRIL** ... Ass, my suster!
> Go kuss him, as the cunning man would have you;
> I'll thrust a pin i' your buttocks else.

The extracts are short enough not to intimidate, and each also gives insight into Jonson's use of language. This is not the 'poetic' language we associate with Shakespeare, but language which tells us HOW a character speaks. Ironically, it is also one of the reasons that Jonson is not better known. Jonson's plays have often been damned because they are not Shakespeare's. The point is that they are different. In Jonson's plays language and action are always theatrically interactive.

4.   *Improvisations based on the opening of the play*

We then moved briefly away from the text itself. The small groups were asked to devise situations for improvisation which would loosely follow the following scenario:

A, B and C have made a plan which involves some kind of illegal activity. They are about to carry it out when A and B start to argue between themselves. Their argument rapidly shifts away from the pros and cons of the plan and becomes increasingly personal. C realises that their argument will prove disastrous and intervenes, attempting to get them both back on course.

The improvisations are played out; and we note the structure of each of the resulting scenes. Where are the climaxes? How does the third character attempt to control the others - verbally and physically?

5.   *Realising the first page of the play*

The first page of the play was then read aloud, and compared with the previous improvisations. This is a strategy for making the reading and interrogation of the playtext as active as possible. Having read the text, it was noted that it is full of 'implied' stage action. In groups of threes, people enacted the scene as actively as possible. This was followed by further discussion about how this modifies thinking/expectation about characters/plot and the whole play.

At this stage in the workshop the large group were divided into small groups, and each of the small groups was given a separate task

6.   Editing and performing act one, scene one

Act One, Scene One is seven pages long. One of the groups was asked to cut this down to about two and a half pages. Having conducted this radical piece of editing (!), they then performed the resulting text. With students who were unfamiliar with the text an exercise like this would take much longer but could be very valuable. When directors approach any Renaissance play they tend to edit it for performance. The act of editing forces you to read the text very carefully, to consider the shape and structure of a scene and of its theatrical functions. The edited text is not definitive, but the act of editing for performance becomes a way of getting to know a text very well. It is in itself an active interrogation of the text and demands that you think about the play as theatre.

One of the joys of working on Jonson is that he is not revered in the way that Shakespeare is. Peter Barnes, a latter day Jonsonian (and himself a vastly underrated playwright), has 'edited' a number of Jonson's plays for performance. In the preface to editions of his own published plays he states very clearly that anybody wanting to perform them SHOULD edit them. The unedited text is there for readers. Theatre audiences need less spoken dialogue as there are so many other signifiers in operation. Peter Barnes is convinced that Jonson himself (who supervised the publication of his own collected works in 1616 - seven years before Shakespeare's plays were published in a Collected Works) expanded his own plays for publication.

7.   Enacting a written summary of act one, scene by scene

One small group were given summaries of the five scenes that make up the first act of the play, and asked to devise a dramatic way of representing this material, so that the ACTION of the first act would be clear to other workshop members.

Extracts from two further short scenes (Act 3, Scene 5 and Act Five, Scene 1) were worked on. Each exemplifies the way that Jonson's dialogue implies stage action.

If we had had more time I would have liked to have worked on Jonson's use of **Alchemy** in *The Alchemist*. This is another example of his extraordinarily playful use of language. The alchemical terms which litter the text are baffling. They make an initial reading of the play potentially perplexing. Consider the following (edited!) extract:

SUBTLE   The work is done; bright *Sol* is in his *robe*.
                    We have a *med'cine* of the *triple soul*,

	The glorified spirit. Thanks to be heaven,	
	And make us worthy of it.	
	Look well to the register,	
	And let your heat still lessen by degrees,	
	To the *aludels* ... Did you look	
	0' the *bolt's head* yet?	

FACE   Which'? On D, sir'?

SUBTLE   Ay.
What's the complexion?

FACE   Whitish.

SUBTLE   Infuse vinegar
To draw his *volatile substance* and his *tincture*,
And let the water in Glass E be filtered.
And put into the *gripe's egg*. Lute him well,
And leave him closed in *balneo*.

FACE   I will, sir.   [*FACE leaves*]

SURLY   What a brave language here is, next to canting!
(Act 2, Scene 3 Lines 29 - 42)

Each of the words in italics is effectively a foreign language. Had we had more time we would have explored the way that the characters might have <u>used</u> this language. What are they <u>doing</u> with the language? How are they making this 'brave language' serve their purposes ... ?

Whenever I have worked on this play with 6th form students they seem to have found it extraordinarily liberating. Here is a great playwright who allows his characters to <u>use</u> language in ways with which they are remarkably familiar. Subtle and Face use the alchemical terms to baffle, to bemuse, to exclude, to impress, to intrigue.

And what pleasure there is in seeing their contemporary parallels: second hand car salesmen, computer buffs, politicians - and teachers. It's good to find a playwright who can show us what we do and make us laugh at ourselves.

Peter Barnes has suggested that the **R**oyal **S**hakespeare **C**ompany should be disbanded and a **R**epublican **J**onson **C**ompany be set up in its place. I'll put my name down as seconder to that motion.

To summarise

The workshops were constructed as a kind of detective game: a detective game which effectively subverts most expectations of the genre; a detective game in which any sense of finite closure is actively denied to the participants; in which participants were given various bits of information to arouse their curiosity about the play, and to encourage them to find their own meanings in it.

(Oh ... and the 'right' answer to the quiz?
Ben Jonson.)

The Sunday workshops

Queer Goings-On in The Cherry Orchard

On the Sunday of the conference, we spent the first of the two workshop sessions on *The Alchemist* again (working on similar material to that described above); and the second of the two on Anton Chekhov's *The Cherry Orchard*.

The rationale for the work was very similar, though the reasons for choosing to work on *The Cherry Orchard* were slightly different. Many students find Chekhov difficult - not because the language is itself difficult but because it's apparently difficult to follow a narrative through-line, difficult to hold on to the characters. Who's who? How on earth do you remember those names?

The first exercise was similar to the early work on *The Alchemist* in that it tries to give students a 'handle' on the material <u>before</u> they start to read the play. The purpose of the following practical exercise is to make it easier for students to identify characters and recognise them as they read the play. Using the list of characters, prepare a formal posed photograph of the characters of the play on the estate. Students simply position themselves in relation to each other and each says aloud the name of the character s/he represents. This may need teacher direction, or it might be an idea to ask the students to skim the text for information to enable them to do the exercise without assistance. With teacher help it might look like this:

- Lyubov stands with Gayev - sister and brother.
- Close to Lyubov is her daughter, Anya, and nearby Varya, her adopted daughter.
  Anya is attended by Charlotta (the governess who has travelled with Lyubov and Anya to Paris). Perhaps watching Anya from a little distance is Petya Trofimov, the student who is awaiting their return.
- Semyonov-Pishchik, the neighbouring landowner, might also be trying to get in on the photograph; but he's not actually part of the family.
- Then there are the four servants: Dunyasha, the young chambermaid, Yepichodov, the estate clerk, Yasha, the young footman who went to Paris with Lyubov, and Firs, the old man who has worked for the family all his life. These four have relationships between themselves, and with the family. But they will be a little way away from the main family group.
- Finally there is Lopakhin, the businessman. Perhaps he has arrived late for the photograph; but is keen to speak to Lyubov.

When they have made the group, each speaks a line or lines from the play aloud which are characteristic in some way. These can come from anywhere in the play. Again, these might be given to the students by the teacher - or they might have to search the text for something which appears to be indicative of character.

Lyubov   Oh my lovely. innocent childhood ... Oh, my dear orchard.

Anya   A whole new world will open up for us.

Varya   I can't bear the thought of having nothing to do ... All this joking. I take it seriously.

Gayev   What I've been through ... How can I refrain from expressing my emotions.

Lopakhin   Done well for meself. Still a peasant though.

Trofimov   The perpetual student it seems ... We must go forward, friends.

Pishchik   Money, money - I never seem to think of anything else ... Lend me two hundred.

Charlotta   I am quite alone ... One more trick.

Firs   I've lived a long time ... In the old days you knew where you were.

Yepichodov   Every day something goes wrong.

Dunyasha   I feel all faint. My hands are trembling.

Yasha   I m not very keen on girls who make fools of themselves ... It's so boring; I'm sure Madame understands.

Having read the play they may want to return to this exercise, organising the characters in other ways; and considering whether there are other lines from the play which are particularly characteristic.

Triangles
We then examined the different possible triangular relationships that exist in the play; and I suggested that it might be productive to see what happens if you consider Yasha, Dunyasha and Yepichodov as the centre of the play. This means looking at the opening of Act Two: an easy scene to play, and potentially one of the more overtly humorous. By shifting the emphasis of the play away

from the aristocracy and on to the more working class characters (if Yasha ever works!) this not only gives quite startling insights into the structure of the play, but also allows us to break with much of the 'established' wisdom about it. It enables teachers who may be quite familiar with the play to see it through unfamiliar eyes. This placing of what is frequently seen as marginal at the centre can be very productive.

Playing across gender

We then extended the idea of placing the marginal at the centre. In small groups people were asked to realise a short extract from the opening of Act Two - but in doing so they had to play across gender: men to play Dunyasha, women to play Yasha and Yepichodov. In each case they were to play the character as the same gender as the actor - so Dunyasha was played as a man.

One group consisted of two men, and they were asked to play Yasha and Dunyasha both as men. The relationship became a gay one. When this scene was played out it created a remarkable sense of danger, and revealed aspects of this scene which are usually hidden from us: the horrible betrayal of Dunyasha that takes place; the riskiness of the relationship, and the audience's complicity in laughing at Yasha's cruelty. All sense of the trivial and the fey had gone. Far from being a play in which not much happens we began to see every relationship as important, the triangles of love, desire and betrayal echoing and resonating throughout the play.

Bibliography

Cave, R. A. (1991). *Ben Jonson*. Macmillan.
Chekhov, A. (1996). *The Cherry Orchard*. Cambridge University Press.
Jonson, B. (1995). *The Alchemist*. Cambridge University Press.
Woolland, B. (1998). *Ben Jonson and the Theatre*. Routledge (forthcoming: October 1998).

Notes

1. Peter Barnes, Edward Bond, John Arden, Charles Dickens have all actively championed Ben Jonson as our great 'unknown' playwright, and all acknowledge a considerable debt to him. Jonson himself wrote an introductory poem for the Folio edition of Shakespeare's collected works.

Grasping the Nettle Where it Stings Most[1]

Geoff Gillham

Geoff Gillham is a playwright and freelance Theatre in Education director.

Mine was the last "keynote address" of the Conference. By the time we arrived at this point on the Sunday morning I judged that what was needed most at this point was not another 'keynote', but rather for teachers themselves to speak - and in doing so in this albeit brief period of time, to allow us all (teachers and non-classroom teachers) to reflect on the difficulty of teaching drama at this moment in time. It was my hope that in effect it would be a 'keynote address' given by the Conference participants themselves.

This written version aims to do two things:
1.　to set out the task that I gave to the participants; and
2.　to offer a description of the methodological thinking behind it.

The second of these - my methodological thinking - was not shared with the participants at the time. What took priority (for me) at the time was <u>a practice for the participants</u>. This written version, in addition to setting out the findings of the participants in the 'keynote', shares some of my methodological thinking with the reader (who may well not have been present at the NATD Conference). Since the Conference 'meta-text' was to consider the extent to which the weekend's activities involved teachers in working with and for their students, energised them, and were appropriate to developing a child-centred humanising curriculum - such a description may be useful beyond the Conference itself.

The 'keynote' task
(a)　Before entering the hall the participants were paired. Those who currently were teaching drama in the classroom were asked to take a slip of purple paper; those not - college lecturers, students, Theatre in Education workers, etc. - to take a slip of green paper. They paired and entered the hall with a partner. The imbalance (of purples) was corrected by pairing the purples and asking one of each pair to function in the task as a green.
(b)　The greens and those purples functioning as greens were asked to do nothing for a few minutes. The purples were asked to:
　　"Recall a recent moment in a drama lesson where you were really at the end of your tether."[2]

I immediately indicated to them that they would not be asked to tell anyone what this moment was. I then asked anyone (of the purples) who could not recall such a moment to raise their hand. (There were perhaps 12 or so of these.) These people I asked to move back from the end of the tether down the continuum to:

"Recall a recent moment in a drama lesson where you were at a loss as to what to do."

A couple of minutes silence then ensued for the recollection.

Methodological observations on (a) and (b)

(a) A disruption of the paradigm of keynote addresses was being signalled. For some this was pleasurable, for others a source of irritation or minor anxiety. The specified division was accepted with equanimity, a slight increase in anxiety about potential self-exposure, or irritation that such a division was being made. The 'negative' features incurred by the paradigm shift were not in my power to prevent - it was only in my power to anticipate the possibility, and to diagnose the quantity and quality of its actual appearance, and to do my best to minimise them. Also signalled from the outset was that we were going to 'get down to business', as it were, "this concerns each and every one of you". Standing on a chair above the 'mêlée' in the vestibule, a firm directorial tone of voice, signalled my control over the situation. For some this was reassuring or energising; for others a source of continuing (or developing) irritation or anxiety - "what is he going to 'make us' do?!".

Over and above the signalling and diagnosis, this section was a means for me of organising a large number of people (160 approx.) as time-efficiently as possible for the task I was to ask them to do <u>before</u> they were asked to do it. Often, and this was a case in point, a teacher/leader wants to be able to move straight to the <u>doing</u> of a task the moment it is set, without that being disrupted by organisational aspects.

(b) On beginning the plenary and offering the title of the 'keynote' - a double-ness is offered: 'danger' and facing 'danger' with the clear indication that facing difficulties is not actually as 'bad' as you may think. The idiomatic nature of the phrasing makes the activity 'septic' as Dorothy Heathcote would say, not dispassionate and anti-septic. By its very language it acknowledges openly the frequent bloodiness of trying to teach authentically and usefully in many schools at the present time. It assumes it. Such things are hard to speak about - our society eschews 'failure' and especially failure of self-control, or failure to cope. Yet such 'failure' (the inverted commas are very important) is ubiquitous and, even more importantly, a rich source of knowledge.

Protection from self-exposure is necessary. Hence the immediate caveat to the task "you will not be asked to tell anyone what the moment was". Similarly, it will be noted the participants were asked to put their hands up (i.e. identify themselves) only if they could <u>not</u> recall such a painful moment. For the latter, the <u>same</u> task was actually offered - formulated by me as a continuum of <u>quantity</u>,

134

but in reality <u>re</u>-formulating the task for a different 'personality-response'.[3]

The task

(c)   The next stage of the task brought in the greens and those functioning as greens. These I told only to ask questions of their partner and not to enter discussion with her/him. They were not to ask <u>directly</u> about the incident recalled by their partner. Their task together was to elicit new knowledge from it. In response to the questioning the purples were asked to try and avoid the following tendencies:

    shame: the tendency to feel guilty about what you did/didn't do;

    blame: the tendency to hold <u>persons</u> (including yourself) responsible for unpleasant sensations in yourself;

    rationalising away: the tendency to avoid considering the real implications and contradictions of something by reaching for ready-made explanations;

    dressing it up with verbiage: the tendency to use high-sounding abstractions in place of concrete analysis.

    making/letting it confirm what you already know: the tendency to impose an impression or interpretation made prior to concrete analysis of the particular phenomenon.

I summarised the reason for asking them to try and avoid these tendencies by saying that I wanted them "to look the animal in the eye". The animal, I hastened to add, was not the kids, but the moment itself and its implications. We were trying to win new knowledge from these painful 'negative' moments.

The question I asked the pairs to address was this:

"What does this moment, on reflection, tell you about:

- the being of those young people?
- the condition of your school?
- the condition of society/the world?
- your own practice/yourself?"

Before they began I asked them to give priority to the first of these categories in the time available. I also made the request and the point that they "respect the discipline of the task. It is not my discipline, but that of the task." About ten minutes, a woefully short time, was given for this.

Methodological observations on (c)

It can now be seen that my control was over the structure and structuring of the task - not over its content. The content was being determined - in this order - by events in the external world, the purples' selection from other possible choices of recent moments on criteria offered by me but interpreted by them, the questions and responses of each member of the pairs, their willingness and ability to 'stay on task'. I think this distinction between power over structuring and power over content-outcome is an important one. Adults, including teachers, can often overlook this distinction. A leader (teacher or theatre director) who takes on the power to structure other people's learning or development is sometimes perceived as seeking to control the content-outcome, i.e. to manipulate the others into agreeing with her/him. This can be the case - although whether successfully, I doubt.

In this session my underlying assumption was that teachers themselves hold the knowledge (a fact little appreciated by governments, inspectors, princes, journalists and - dare I say? not a few college lecturers in education) about the nature of teaching in these times. Our social effort is to bring this knowledge first to the teacher's own consciousness and then to the social consciousness of the Conference, and beyond. Winning this knowledge is as difficult and as skilled an operation as winning coal. The same is true of teaching young people: they know more closely than we the nature of being young and being a learner in these times. The task I set the pairs was geared to their trying to win this new knowledge from teachers' own difficulties with the act of teaching them in the drama room.

It was noticeable (not only to me) how difficult the pairs found it to 'stay on task' and to 'obey its discipline'. This is not a criticism. Or rather, not a criticism of the participants. Our society does not encourage us to study problems and difficulties carefully. It does not encourage us to study things, processes, events in a scientific or disinterested way. It does not encourage us to reflect upon our experiences and the feelings they often engender at the time of having them. It does not encourage us to adopt a cool strip, or to develop what Dorothy Heathcote has called "the self-spectator" (I am in the action and reflecting upon it.). Our society encourages - in practice, if not by words - raw emotion and alienated thinking (impressionism, speculation, etc.) and separates them (emotion and thinking) absolutely from each other. Each, and the separation of emotion and thought, creates madness in our society and disempowerment with respect to truly solving difficulties and problems. In such circumstances, morality and oppressiveness come to the fore and substitute themselves for real solutions.

The task I offered ran counter to this form of insanity. The strong emotion is the means to locate an objectively existent problem. It is not the emotion which is studied but its source in the objective world - including the self: the four categories. The problem is considered concretely, in its particularity, but the categories taken as a whole (I think rightly) pre-suppose that the source of the problem lies principally outside the personal control of the individual teacher; that is to say, it has universal significance or manifests a universal. (It will be noticed that only after studying those categories external to the teacher herself, were the participants asked to consider what the incident illuminated about the teacher's own practice.)

I believe that contradictorily this approach to problems is empowering.

It is empowering to understand what I cannot as an individual change - but which by implication <u>may</u> be changed by social action. It is empowering to isolate that which I can as an individual change once having found what it is. This provides the <u>only</u> condition for an appropriate search for the means to change it, i.e., methodology and specific strategies of practice.[4]

The task

(d)   The work of the pairs was then halted and the pairs were asked to spend a few minutes to formulate a couple of sentences, to express something from their consideration they felt was an important piece of new knowledge to share in plenum.

(e)   Before beginning the sharing in the plenary I asked each contributor to preface their brief statement with one of the following rubrics:
        "It is the case that ...."
        "I/We think that probably ...."
        "I/We have the feeling that it might be that ...."

The sharing began with the first category, and moved through each of the categories in the order given. There were perhaps twenty contributions in the course of the following ten or fifteen minutes. I made no comment upon them, with the exception of an early one which spoke of "some schools". I interjected, "Speak only of <u>your</u> school. Try not to generalise".

Methodological observations on (d) and (e)

A priority for me was to have time for as many contributions as possible in the plenary. It will be noticed that in (d) I asked only for a couple of sentences, and not a summary: I wanted us to look at each new piece of coal, not a coal heap. <u>(e)</u> was the coal heap which the participants made with their bits of coal. Such an approach privileged the less confident (in speaking in large plenaries) while keeping those, like me, who can chunter on in generalities in check! Everyone kept to this discipline, which in my view is remarkable.

Less remarkable was the fact that few of the contributors used one of the offered prefatory rubrics. I made the decision, as this became apparent, not to 'insist' upon this form. I judged it was more important to allow as much as possible of the content of the contributions to come into the social domain, than to spend time pressing for the discipline of the task and risking at this closing point of the plenary the activation of feelings of inexpertness ("not doing it right").

However it is worth noting that the intention of the prefatory rubrics was three-fold:

(1)   to heighten the significance of the contributions through an element of formalised ritual;

(2)   and therefore to shift the quality of listening;

(3)   to acknowledge and support equally the different phases or kinds of

knowledge - that which <u>asserts</u> on the basis of evidence understood, that which while tentative is a <u>useful hypothesis for further consideration,</u> and <u>intuitive knowledge</u> which may not yet be proved empirically or not be able on the basis of empirical evidence to be proved, yet which by retaining contact with sensuous and subliminal understanding may well be very close to genuinely new insights/knowledge.[5]

Underlying this desire for as many contributions as possible and my insistence on the pairs and contributions being concrete and particular, was that through this process we could hear the emergence of the universal(s) contained in each incident but only truly cognisable as such through the appearance of the connections and interconnections - the pattern or law - in each. Only when we do this can we really break from treating problems as '<u>my</u> problem' or indeed 'someone <u>else's</u> problem' . All problems in the end are social problems. The problem is to identify their true nature - which can only come by studying the problems themselves. The proper study of a problem, i.e. its full analysis, by yielding up its own nature (as a negative) delineates the nature of its solution (as a negative of the negative, i.e. a positive). Thus, the title of our "keynote": grasping the nettle tightly prevents one from being stung by it.

Notes

1. The stinging nettle (Urtica Dioica) is a common European herbaceous plant which is often seen on urban waste-ground as well as in hedgerows, woodland, and farmland. The stalk and under-leaves are covered by minute hairs which are irritants when touched or brushed against. It is the foodplant of many insect species, including the small tortoiseshell butterfly larvae. Gardeners of former times grew it between currant and other soft-fruit bushes. Whether this was to keep children away or to feed the soil with nitrogen, silica, iron, protein, phosphates, formic acid and other mineral salts excreted by the nettles' roots I do not know. Young nettles, cooked in the manner of spinach, are delicious and very nutritious - and needless to say lose their capacity to sting in the cooking. How much richness there is in a plant which at first touch produces a very unpleasant sensation!

2. For the non-British reader it may be useful to say that to be "at the end of one's tether" is a common idiom meaning "to lose all patience, being nearly out of control". A domestic animal is tethered when it is tied by a rope or chain to a stake driven into the ground.

3. To use the terms in the way offered by Dorothy Rowe as "the preference each of us has for internal or external reality", the first formulation ('end of

tether') is the formulation for introverts (and perhaps the most 'dramatic'). The second formulation ('at a loss what to do') is the formulation for extroverts. It is indeed a continuum, but not one of quantity so much as one of quality (of subjective respc　　　　　　ternal reality). See Dorothy Rowe: "The Successful Self", 1988

4. Before leaving the question of　　　　　　respecting the discipline of the task', it is im　　　　　　tasks were not within a drama or fictive frame.　　　　　　to stay on task is provided by the dramatic　　　　　　to respect the discipline of the task is provid　　　　　　nd investments in relation to the task. With　　　　　　g on task and respecting its discipline are　　　　　　on, will, and ability - all 'subjective' chara　　　　　　ie participants were being asked to respect m　　　　　　ied) discipline in the form of respecting the　　　　　ke in drama - Mantle of the Expert for example, there was no ongoing support or scaffolding external to them even if they wished initially to carry through the task as offered.

5. A similar point can be made as in n.4. This was not in a fictive/drama context which can create the need for such formalised speech, felt by the participants.